CLASSIFICATION: POETRY

A CIP catalogue record for this book is available from
the British Library.

Printed and bound in Great Britain.

Cover photograph of Torquay harbour by Gregory
Paul.

Paper used in the production of books published by
United Press comes only from sustainable forests.

This Northern Ireland, Isle of Man, Wales and North West
England edition

ISBN 1-84436-234-5

First published in Great Britain in 2005 by
United Press Ltd
Admail 3735
London
EC1B 1JB
Tel: 0870 240 6190
Fax: 0870 240 6191
ISBN for complete set of volumes
1-84436-237-X
All Rights Reserved

*www.unitedpress.co.uk*

# Perfectly Poetic

4

# Foreword

Is it possible to achieve perfection in a poem? To do so, the author must realise that perfect blend of subject, style, presentation, interpretation and expression.

He or she must explore the heights and depths of his or her own personality, experiences, passions, abilities, and, probably most importantly, his or her own humanity.

It is the human side of our nature that makes poetry so important. Poetry is there to explore and try to understand human nature - in all its imperfections and glories.

I don't think the perfect poem will ever be written but I am sure that every poet will still strive to achieve perfection in their work.

That is why I am delighted to be able to present you, the reader, with this compilation of work by so many different poets, all of whom see as their goal the quest to be *Perfectly Poetic.*

*Peter Quinn, Editor*

# Contents

The poets who have contributed to this volume are listed below, along with the relevant page upon which their work can be found.

| | | | |
|---|---|---|---|
| 61 | Rosemarie Parry | 96 | Jenny Lomax |
| 62 | Anthony Hillier | | Geoffrey W Lever |
| 63 | Marliese Porter | 97 | Oliver Waterer |
| 64 | George Kaine Baker | 98 | Susan Middlehurst |
| 65 | Annie Morrisey | 99 | James Barnes |
| 66 | David Jacks | | Marion Kaye |
| | Dawn Hough | 100 | Mumtaz Ali |
| 67 | Celia Cholmondeley | 101 | Maureen Williams |
| | Liz Standish | | Iris Tennent |
| 68 | M Munro Gibson | 102 | Christine Dickinson |
| 69 | Philip John Savage | 103 | J E Offord |
| 70 | Edna Fallowfield | | Natalie Rowlands |
| | Jones | 104 | Anthony C Griffiths |
| 71 | Damian Mitchell | 105 | Dawn Prestwich |
| | Kathryn Butler | | Elsie Ryan |
| 72 | John Evans | 106 | Edith Smith |
| 73 | John Crotty | 107 | Colin Foe |
| 74 | Nicole Broad | | Angela Priest |
| 75 | Gemma Connell | 108 | Gillian Hesketh |
| 76 | Jenni J Moores | 109 | Clifford Chambers |
| | Barbara Ellison | 110 | Eric Dodgson |
| 77 | Gill Pomfret | | Sophie Wenborn |
| 78 | Diana Burrows | 111 | Constance Price |
| 79 | Eve Armstrong | 112 | Stuart Whitham |
| 80 | Jane Parker | 113 | Janet Hosler |
| 81 | Diane Stanley | 114 | Anantha Rudravajhala |
| 82 | Annette Smith | | Kathleen Frances West |
| | Brian Perry | 115 | Jo Rainford |
| 83 | Anthony Clements | 116 | Valerie Wyatt |
| 84 | Sylvia Quayle | 117 | Kelly Morgan |
| 85 | Laura Boustead | 118 | Marie Kay |
| | Christopher Hall | 119 | Alice Campbell |
| 86 | Dawn Graham | | Barbara Jardine |
| 87 | Angela Robinson | 120 | Eileen Hudson |
| 88 | Brian D Lancaster | 121 | Amy Hawkins |
| 89 | Julia Dent | 122 | Sheila Baldwin |
| | Richard Clark | | Greg Foley |
| 90 | Marlene Allen | 123 | Sheila Ellis |
| 91 | Brian Campbell | 124 | Peter Hewitt |
| 92 | Ben Almond | 125 | Tanya Sorell |
| 93 | Brian Capps | 126 | Peter Lang |
| 94 | William Smyth | | Katherine Fish |
| 95 | Patricia Spear | 127 | Paul Burton |

| | | | |
|---|---|---|---|
| 128 | Elizabeth Holt | | McBrier |
| 129 | Mavis Ann Abrahams | 160 | Kathryn Evans |
| 130 | Briony O'Callaghan | 161 | John Dancey |
| | Pamela Igoe Hall | 162 | Joan Conway |
| 131 | Ian Hogg | 163 | Doug Smith |
| 132 | Eileen Waldron | 164 | Leanne Victoria Evans |
| 133 | Jean Wood | 165 | Chrissie Taylor |
| 134 | Josie Carter | | Reginald Waywell |
| 135 | Marjorie Pinder | 166 | Ann Marie Whitehouse |
| 136 | Jim Haslam | 167 | Megan Ingham |
| 137 | Andrew Hughes | | Jenna Fye |
| 138 | Doris Thomson | 168 | Geoff Hunter |
| 139 | Margaret Howarth | 169 | Clare Bell |
| | Paul Neads | 170 | Chrys Valentine |
| 140 | Simon Bostock | | Hannah Schofield |
| | Ann Noble | 171 | Charlotte Bevis |
| 141 | Freda Grieve | 172 | Suzanne Jenkinson |
| 142 | Gemma Dutton | 173 | Ann Sutcliffe |
| 143 | Amanda Johnson | 174 | Margaret O'Neil |
| 144 | Tracy Costello | 175 | Margery Mahon |
| | Marj Kurthausen | 176 | Mary J Baxter |
| 145 | Martha Birch | 177 | Carmel Allison |
| 146 | Penny Wilson | 178 | Andrea Davies |
| | Jean-Angela Smith | 179 | Jean Broadhurst |
| 147 | Kim-Marie Fisher | | Stephen Mitton |
| 148 | Thomas McCabe | 180 | George Donnellan |
| | Albert Pearson | | Elizabeth Porter |
| 149 | Christine Hale | 181 | David Shepherd |
| 150 | Wendy Black | 182 | Jacqui Dunne |
| | Suzanne Strain | | |
| 151 | Lynn Kilpatrick | | |
| 152 | Philip Johnson | | |
| | Meleeze Zenda | | |
| 153 | Hilary McShane | | |
| 154 | Ann Blair | | |
| | Elizabeth Browne | | |
| 155 | Janet Hagen | | |
| | Paul Hutton | | |
| 156 | Samuel Coulter | | |
| 157 | Julieann Campbell | | |
| 158 | Rose-Mary Gower | | |
| | Kiera Patricia Byrne | | |
| 159 | Derrick Alexander | | |

# SONG OF THE RIVER

The river is deep the river is wide,
Taking everything in its stride
As it flows gently along,
Listen to its haunting song.

Down through valleys, up through dales,
Under bridges on it sails,
Never no time to look around
At all the beauty that can be found.

Going on and on forever,
Getting stronger, stopping never,
Free as a bird released from its cage
Till it reaches its final stage.

Then at last its journey's end
Is in sight and round the bend,
As it sighs and waits to be
United fully with the sea.

*Sandra Boyde, Belfast, Northern Ireland*

**Sandra Boyde** said: "I have been writing poetry for about
five years. I get great pleasure writing, I have had about six
or seven poems published. My three daughters give me
great inspiration. I like cinema, dancing and foreign holi-
days. I am an auxiliary nurse in a local hospital and really
enjoy my work. I am also a care worker in an old people's
home and love looking after them. They also influence me a
lot. I love to express myself through poetry and hope people
get pleasure reading it."

## LOVE'S CRUCIBLE

Go fetch your canvas, paint and brush,
Paint these images, brushstrokes don't rush.
Paint a landscape hung with solitude
With misery in the air. Where I am stood
Create my silhouette in a misty blue
Like a ghost or a shadow, grey in hue.

Let a foreboding shiver saturate the air,
The mourning sky darken, where I stand there.
Make teardrops tumbling to the ground
Amidst wind and rain and paint the sound,
Make colours of sadness and sorrow run
Throughout the picture and have no sun.

Paint pain emblazoned on a bleeding heart,
Beating alone now that he and I are apart.
When you've finished and the painting's dry
Make sure the tears in my eyes still cry,
Then all who look at the picture will remember
How I burned in love's crucible that September.

*Joan Magennis, Belfast, Northern Ireland*

OLD TOOLS

Useless without his strong hand on the wooden handle,
The hammer he could pick from a dozen blindfolded
Lies sulking in the toolbox like a neglected friend,
The once polished steel head now pitted with rust,
While sunk in the earth surrounded by wood an old pal
turns to dust.

*Gerard McSorley, Belfast, Northern Ireland*

THE RIVER BANN, BANBRIDGE

It is in thought I wander
To the place where I was born,
Where autumn leaves colour September
And like serene music
Flows the river Bann.

At the Mantovani ripple of the river,
Bough the trees in regal elegance,
While the falling leaves dance
Upon the water
And the trout rise, each endearing note to catch.

Idyllic beneath her bridge she
Nestles daily,
Attentively listening to the wheels of time
Embracing affectionately, lane ways in
The distance
That stray through the hollow, prominent
In Banbridge town.

*Elizabeth Aulds, Banbridge, Northern Ireland*

YOU ALREADY KNOW

An interview for the job
That you do not want
But "must do", is a good master.
The waiting
In wasted space,
The reception,
The hanging pictures,
Modern art,
Over, under-used,
Suites of furniture
That will probably be replaced
Soon.
That factory
That you often passed,
Ignored,
But subconsciously classed
Beneath you,
Now above you
Produces things, that others need,
But no-one more needy
Than you.

*Stephen Breen, Lurgan, Northern Ireland*

NEW BEGINNINGS

Soft flakes flutter on frozen ground
transforming the Wirral for your arrival.

First mewling cries captivate, overwhelm,
Hair of thistledown, eyes of ocean-blue.

Bathed in snow shine, cradled in cotton,
You suckle and drowse, lighting our lives.

*Mary Hayward, Limavady, Northern Ireland*

BEHIND THE BARS

I'm sitting here, yapping
Watching the world go by
From my pen.
My neighbours are noisy
And bigger than me;
Faces, human, I'm told
Look and pass by.
Days become weeks,
Weeks, months,
I'm still here.
The alsatian has gone.
Then
A golden-haired child
Stops,
Looks straight into my eye
Saying
Will you come home with me?
I'm jumping here, happy.

*Hazel Moore, Douglas, Isle of Man*

## AUTUMN TWILIGHT

Soft shimmering shadows
Hover round his chair,
Pink and purple twilight
Lingers in his lair.

Sweet scent of roses
Permeates the room,
Summer's gone and autumn
Soon will ply her broom.

Old man musing
As the night draws nigh,
Fills his pipe and contemplates
The quiet evening sky.

Pausing for a little while
Before the leaves come down,
Reflects upon the golden store
And waits the bronze and brown.

Resting at this peaceful hour
With dreams of yesterday,
Listens for the autumn winds
Old age's wintry lay.

*Arlene Allen, Banbridge, Northern Ireland*

Born in Belfast **Arlene Allen** has interests including reading, writing, walking and crosswords. "I started writing poetry when I was four and my work is influenced by many of the major poets and the people I meet on the Cornish coastline. I spend six months of every year in our home in Cornwall," she explained. "I would describe my style as lyrical and I would like to be remembered as someone who cared about people and animals." Aged 66, Arlene is from the teaching profession and has an ambition to write a bestselling novel. She is married to David and has written many poems, several of which have been published.

UNTITLED

If poetry is a dance then we are its dancers,
If music is a painting then we are its artists,
If love is an emotion then we are its creators.
We can be more than great,
We will be more than great,
We already are.

*Linda Elizabeth Rose Smith, Cookstown, Northern Ireland*

*Dedicated to Ian, for all we grew to become in each other's eyes, Tinkerbell and Peter Pan.*

BETWEEN TWO HEARTS

The distance between two hearts
Is measured not in words of creed
Where God and Allah
Vie to take the upper hand,
Nor is it measured by a debt of culture
When the rhythms of its beat
Are swallowed up by ritual
And obligation.
The distance between two hearts
Is measured always in our love
Where every bridge we cross
Becomes a treasured memory
Of what we gave and gained
Together through our lives
And if we listen closely
We will hear its echo
Touch another's heart
As you touched mine and always let me fly.

*Lynda Tavakoli, Lisburn, Northern Ireland*

# FLOWERS IN THE DUST

No more
The communal fire
Orange flames dancing
Over red hot coals
Embracing all before it

No more
The rhythmic
Ticking of the clock
The lethargic
Chime on the hour

No more
The flowers
Sitting in a vase
Scent drifting
Through the room

No more
The home that lives
And breathes
Now just a house
Of memories

*Ivan Wallace, Carrickfergus, Northern Ireland*

# REFLECTIONS

Fond embraces and merriment far in the past,
Suppressed in the memory - the heartaches outlast
Her years by the sea, four score and more
In a seafaring family that lived by the shore.

Rippling tide and the sun on the wave,
Recurring reflections of a watery grave,
Scars on her mind like the dark clothes she wore,
Walking the water's edge down by the shore.

Her shadow for company no sunshine to give,
A solitary figure her days to outlive,
Those whom she knew all gone before,
How lonely now life by a permanent dark shore.

Seemed she'd always been there, the same daily grind,
Then one day she's gone no trace left behind,
Belatedly all ask could we have done for her more,
That little old lady who lived by the shore.

Taking only her grief where now could she be
To rest with dear loved ones as she walked out to sea,
For their loss long ago was the cross that she bore,
Her broken heart with them away out on the shore.

*William Donaldson, Holywood, Northern Ireland*

## WHITE STAR MADNESS

Off she sailed in her glory
Across the Irish Sea,
The biggest ship ever seen, she was
the size of three.
Now the White Star line got greedy,
they said increase the speed,
the captain he cried out to them,
Surely there's no need,
But they offered him a bonus
To break the record time
All for the good name of
the greedy White Star line.

*Victor Blain, Carrowdore, Northern Ireland*

## ABSENCE

A house, a room with vacant ground,
Feeling loneliness all around.
A sense of loss, an emptiness inside,
An obvious absence - no more by my side.
The voice, a feature, the face, just a look,
To comfort and console me, that's all that it took.
An item here, a belonging there,
A cardigan covering an empty chair,
A cooker, a sink and a table are all simple reminders of you
As your teapot, your mug and your table cloth, are still in
clear view.
How sadly missed you are, our family will never be the
same again,
Life goes on I know, so our longing is all in vain.
Nothing will be normal or the way things used to be,
Your house is not our home now, and it's never going to be.

*Lynn Paston, Lisburn, Northern Ireland*

CHRISTMAS

Thank you God for Christmastime
For your only begotten Son,
Thank you God for Christmas,
For the presents and the fun.

Thanks for all the children,
their delight on Christmas morn,
Thank you God for Christmas Day,
The day your Son was born.

Thanks for all the neighbours
Who greet us with a smile,
Thanks for those who care for us
And make our lives worthwhile.

We hope and pray that some day
All the bitterness and strife
Will disappear around us
And we'll enjoy a better life.

Thank you God for everything
You on our lives bestow
And please look down upon us
And guide us here below.

*Robert McClements, Carrickfergus, Northern Ireland*

IN THIS LIFE

I am a river of flowing emotions
Never stopping in this life

Theoretically testing obstacles
Hurtling headlong over heaving hurdles
I seek the stillness of silent pools
Saddling the soft banks

Leaving reluctantly the second source
In caverns high imperceptible beginnings
Flow in a trickle I
Envelop a new infinity

*Genevieve Haire-Crudden, Magheraveeley, Northern Ireland*

LIFE AT SEA

Yes, I've sailed aboard that
Ship of broken dreams
On that timeless sea
Of hope and shattered schemes,

But, then some day
I may catch a poem
That's gone astray
In those waters of my dismay.

Then, I'll call it my own
And with that I'll pay
For all the time
That's ebbed and flowed away.

*Kenn Norris, Newtown Abbey, Northern Ireland*

GOOSEBERRY BUSH

This weed-struck yard was once a tidy plot,
Collage of salad, roots and summer fruit,
But gentle gardeners' care and love could not
Prevent disorder caused by time's pursuit.

The musty scent under the hot-house glass
Lingers, where plump tomatoes swelled, grew hot.
The panes are broken, wood is splintered, grass
Grows thick. The vines, the apples turn and rot.

A bulging wooden keg, which used to cradle
Bloated strawberries, sits mournfully at the door.
Its steel-drum partner lists, but still it ladles
Rain collected from the guttering floor.

The broken fence records the painful places
Where childhood play occasioned falls and spills
And blood on shins and tears on reddened faces
Were wiped away and cleaned by Grandad's skills.

And tucked away amongst the ragged, lush
And overactive foliage gone awry,
Remains a single hardy gooseberry bush.
Your birthplace, Grandad said, with crinkling eye.

*Arthur Greenwood, Bangor, Northern Ireland*

# THE GLENS OF ANTRIM

The glens are a colourful view
They are quite a few.
They are nine
of hilly kind.

Glenarm glen of the army,
Glencloy glen of the dykes
where you cycle your bikes.

Glenariff of the plough,
Horse and plough little of them now.
Glenballyemon Edwardstown glen
with winding bend.
Glenaan, glen of the ford
where they once used swords.
Glencorp glen of the dead,
spooky they said.
Glendun brown glen nice run,
Glenshesk glen of the reeds
where they sow their seeds.
Glentaisie Rathlin Princess name Taisie,
That sounds crazy.
They all have fame
In their name.

*Marie Coyles, Dervock, Northern Ireland*

# THE OLD COUNTRY STORE

As I drove past the derelict old country store
On a cold and wintry night,
My mind took me back to the days of my youth
When I'd gasp at the wondrous sights
Of bacon and ham and home made jam
And sacks of loose lentils and peas,
Brown salted ling, now that was the thing
To have for our Sunday tea.

Large muslin wrapped cheese, with dark yellow rind
Sat on thick marble slabs next to sardines in brine,
Large tea chests with silver foil linings
And sugar in brown paper bags,
All behind a mahogany counter
Which had scratches and grooves, and it sagged.

Glass domes, covered tasty "iced diamonds" away from wee
fingers and flies,
Beside them were "black jacks" and "sherbets" and lots of
"cream chocolate Fry's".

The smells of that shop never leave me and they can't be
replaced anymore,
For modernisation and hygiene
Were the end, for the old country store.

*Shirley Gault, Carrickfergus, Northern Ireland*

POEMS

Poetry passes the time of time,
Doodling with words is the only way,
Jotting, juggling as my mind gets to work,
It is funny how sometimes an idea lurks.
Sometimes when washing or ironing maybe
I just have to stop, or I forget you see,
Many a time I've got up out of bed
To find a pen and paper before dropping into zeds.
When my mind goes into overdrive
Time and place don't matter, I feel alive,
Thoughts start slowly, then suddenly abound
Words all shapes and sizes go round and round.
Writing a poem is a pastime to me
But seeing them in print, just fills me with glee.

*Carole Cheetham, Onchan, Isle of Man*

THE TABLE OF LIFE

At the table of life
Good flows in abundance,
Dreams are bought and borrowed
For a day of vision,
I am under this table
Waiting for the crumbs to fall
In to my outstretched hands
So that I can pass them on
To weary travellers.
Minds seeking a chance to prosper and grow,
Never worry.
The table groans with weight
There are no collapsing legs here
Everyone is free to run and take.

*Jean Gardner, Belfast, Northern Ireland*

LIFE IS A FLOWER

The scent of a wild rose,
The aroma of a sweet perfume,
I watch in awe the flower bloom.

Life is like a flower
Precious in your hand.
Let the petals unfold,
Travel across the land.

True beauty is in the eye of the beholder
And like the flower we too must grow older.

Eventually the flower will wither and die,
Make the most of your time before life passes you by.

*Lee-Ann Dalton, Belfast, Northern Ireland*

A PEACEFUL DAY

I took my boat out to fish one day
And dropped my anchor down,
I cast my line over the side
It was just a perfect day.
As time passed by and not one bite
I lay down to rest,
Gazing into the bright blue sky
Not one cloud could I see.
As I floated in my boat
There was nothing but peace all around,
It could have been Heaven I was in
Except for just one thing,
The bell on my fishing rod
Just began to ring.
Ah, what a peaceful day.

*Pamela Coffey, Belfast, Northern Ireland*

## POETIC JUSTICE

'Twas Joe's ninety-second birthday
So he went out to celebrate.
His friends were all so generous,
He got well over the eight.

A woman at the table said
You're just a drunken lout.
My God, you're an ugly woman,
Said Joe, without a doubt.

The woman looked at Joe and said,
You ought to see yourself,
A real disgrace for all to see
You haven't any sense.

Now just you think about it ma'am
I may be somewhat toper,
But though I may be drunk tonight
Tomorrow I'll be sober.

*Maureen Quirey, Antrim, Northern Ireland*

THE VOICE

John the song, the voice, rings a bell;
Once upon a time, disabled, now he's healed.
Wonderful lord of love, a story to tell.
Accident, many years ago, wheel chair then required,
Twelve years with witnesses to prove the truth.
Young mans before and after story to inspire,
Stricken, wounded, disabled, for such has always been.
Are you one healed, when all else failed,
Perhaps inspired, must tell now, heard or seen.
I was there, 'twas my son; the voice.
From faith of believing, to faith of knowing,
Life reborn. Thanks be to God. Praise rejoice.

Going to run he said, steady I replied,
No. Show you hundred yards, blew my mind,
Ran back; glory be to God I cried.
Presence of holy spirit in church close by,
Came home to fetch you, John told me,
Prayed, ran, didn't fall, felt he could, fly.
Sings and dances now, cabaret and TV.
All is with God. Amen, Let it be.

*John Henry Evans, Porthcawl, Wales*

**John Henry Evans** said: "I have been known as Jack since birth. I'm widowed and blessed with a loving family. As a World War II veteran I am a member of the Royal British Legion. A retired engineer I have been writing poetry 60 years. I've waited a long time for John's story in print - Miracle? Some seen but not believed, some not seen but heard, believed. All is in God's hands. Poetry frequently opens doors to new friendships. I pray *The Voice* will open the door to God's kingdom for those in need. I believe my darling Marjorie and I will meet again. Thanks be to God for all his goodness, I look forward to ultimate revelation."

## OUR FAITH

In a land far away on a day long ago
A special babe was born,
We knew him then we know him now
As Jesus Christ our Lord.

It matters not what race we are
We all are his dear children,
He knows of all the good and bad
And forgives without condition.

As our dear Lord passed through the years
Towards his destiny,
He taught his people how to love
And how to serve unselfishly.

So now the cross is ours to bear
To carry on his teachings,
To show the people's of this world
The way to their salvation.

*Mary Cole, Penarth, Wales*

# I AM A POET

I am a poet
I am very fond of berries.
I am berries
I am very fond of a poet.
I am a poet of berries
Very berry mad.
A fond poet of, yes, yes, I am
Very berries.
Fond I am of berries
I am a very poet.
Poet, berries, rich ripe berries
I am fond of a poet.
I am a poet of very red berries
I am a poet.

*Susan Peach, Colwyn Bay, Wales*

# DAWN AT COSMETAN LAKES

Fingers of golden light pierce May's dewy mists
The rippling water glistening like diamonds.
Under the widening azure virgin white swans
Shepherd clusters of velvet grey progeny in majestic
Splendour.

Regal herons haunt the forest of reeds
Beneath the chilly waters shoal of red fin flit here and
There,
Wary of dark pools where predatory pike lurk

In warming shadows by the waters edge
Midges dance and swifts and swallows twist and turn
Playful squirrels scurry from tree to tree,
And timid rabbits chew dew rich grass.

*Ewart Richards, Penarth, Wales*

## NO GREATER GIFT DO I HAVE

No greater gift do I have than you,
A radiant soul that shines through,
Like summer breeze that stirs the senses,
So patiently you dissolved my defenses.

No stronger feelings of love have I known,
Until now my heart always sailed alone,
Like the rising of dawn when the suns on fire,
You have warmed my body with your desire.

No words could ever express what you mean to me,
For you are the air that enables me to breathe,
Like a sailor fighting the monsters of the sea,
You are the light that reached out to guide me.

No regrets will ever enter this thankful heart,
Even if our souls should have to part,
You have given so much of you to me,
I will always be near even when your soul flies free.

*Emma Owen, Flint, Wales*

COMPANION?

If there is no one there,
Then you are quite alone.
Why this feeling of company
That someone other hovers
On the edge, on the periphery.
Turn to catch a glimpse, and it's gone.
Try to describe what you see
From the corner of your eye.
Sometimes, a comfort, a happy chance.
Others, unease that it might be a nod
Or a hint to delay or desist,
Even though when common sense insists
There is no one there
At all.

*Jean Greenall, Mold, Wales*

A GOODNIGHT TO MY SON

It will be yours,

Rain that does not wet you, midnight sun from your eyes.
The game of falling in love, deep pain of the first goodbye.
You will heal your heart, in the splendid, ruthless youth.
I will be in the front row, when you sing that
Christmas is beautiful because is cold outside.
I will hide when you're embarrassed by me.
I will wait in the long night, when you'll be warrior
Conqueror of the world
But, for the moment goodnight, night thief.
Me so eager to steal, from your tender cheeks
A moment of peace
A minute of you
The eternity of us.

*Michele Mennitto, Neath, Wales*

# DON'T LEAVE JUST YET

Silence comes between us,
But words are not important,
I try to find the right words to say,
But as I speak they choke me and die away.

You look at me as if you know,
You hold on to my hand, it's so cold.
Your eyes are empty but full of pain,
I wish for one moment I could take that away.

I'm frightened to hold you in my arms,
And that you'll go away,
To tell you the things I never say
I love you dad and I will every day.

I know your going to leave me,
That's a fact I got to face.
But please don't leave just yet dad,
No one could ever fill your place.

*Haley Pritchard, Pontycymer, Wales*

# WORLD WAR ONE POEM

Smoke and fire, bombs and blood,
In the field shrapnel is spread,
Plastered all over no mans land,
My broken friends are lying dead.

They chose to fight for their country,
They volunteered, they fought,
Then there's Haig, with his luxury,
For his troops, there was no thought.

Confused and blindfolded, walking in a line,
Distressed, not knowing if they'll survive,
Back home, they think of fun and good times,
The joy of returning back to their wives.

Back here in the trenches,
This is all but a dream,
My life is trapped in this war,
I'm going to die here it seems.

*Rhonwen Ebsworth, Pendine, Wales*

## DOWN A WINDY ROAD

Daisies bent backward by a sudden gust,
Mice hide their heads, choked by the dust.

Here's where we walked that sunny day,
Hand in hand, eyes aglow, heart-strings at play.

My heart cried, hang onto your joy unsurpassed.
Then love slipped and was gone. Why didn't it last?

As the wind dances down this lonely path,
I see you swept from me. Goodbye to your laugh;

Goodbye to your traits: your walk and your smile.
Farewell, the wind blows. I'll forget for a while.

*Meredith Vallis, Pontypool, Wales*

## SOMETHING

Something I can't remember and never want to forget,
How the moon affects us all and the sun
Will always set.

Always deep inside me cutting
Like a knife, is something that's always
Haunting me, that something is my life.

Sometimes I can let it go,
Sometimes I just cry, always without reason,
Never knowing why.

Someone who can tell me things that I want
To hear.
Others will never know the meaning of true fear.

*Leanne Childs, Merthyr Tydfil, Wales*

LONGING FOR A CALL

Would you think some more of me if I were fervent not
In all the ways I think of you and never have forgot
How much your life it means to me then onwards as we go
Would you be more caring if I never let you know
How very much you're thought of as I go from day to day
In wondering what you're doing at your work and in your play
And longing for a call so I could ask and you might tell
That happiness is in your heart and you are keeping well
But if you never call it doesn't matter all the same
I'll carry on my thoughts about your life and say your name
Each time I go to sleep at close of day then I will dream
Of fond romance and how our lives together might have been

*Stephen Paul, Porthmadog, Wales*

CORNERS

This is the house I lived in for five years
from the age of nothing until four,
after which I left to join a circus
where I was taught to do my homework
by Charly Corolli's cousin.
When the rains turned up
and the people stayed away,
we'd eat lemon cake and stare at our feet
until our eyes became blurry.
Haircuts and baths were necessary
but not welcome
until the day I discovered girls and dancing.

I still don't eat the crusts off bread.

*Gareth Wyn Davies, Gorslas, Wales*

# THEY DON'T RECOGNISE THE NAME OF ALI APPARENTLY

It was a telephone text message to her friend:
Still in immigration in Florida after six hours, they don't
recognise the name of Ali apparently and a hurricane fast
approaching.
A trip of a lifetime, paid for by remortgage to take her
parents back to Jamaica.
Stuck in immigration for six hours, how long did they end
up waiting?
Did they ever get out of immigration and on their way?
Anyone with a name that does not conform held in
immigration.
No wonder the parents had never returned home.
Terrorists would have all the right documents, would have
the right names,
But Ali was not recognised, an elderly couple and their
daughter treated like criminals.
This is what we have become, paranoid beyond belief,
The computer does not recognise the name of Ali
apparently.

*Melanie M Burgess, Aberystwyth, Wales*

CHOCOLATE

I used to be your chocolate,
Held in tender fingertips,
Eyes devoured me, bright alive.
Unwrapped with hungry searching hands.
Placed to soft warm lips,
Melt in your mouth so sweet,
Enjoyed each bite, with lust,
Hunger quenched, a satisfying end.

I used to be your chocolate.
Now a crumpled wrapper,
Lost your love of chocolate,
Lost a love to love.

*Iain Lewis, Wrexham, Wales*

STORM

The rain in Spain is nothing to the rain in Wales.
Yesterday in Cwmbran it shot right through the sky
Like fighter jets bent on destruction.
Wind roared, whistled, whipped at fragile roofs
And made them scream.
Terrified I rushed to M&S,
Implored St Michael keep me safe.
But once inside the store the atmosphere was calm
The wretched weather was no more.
Docile mothers drifted in a dream,
Their children craved all that they could see.
Well-fed women filled their bags with food they did not
need.
Young girls bought tights and frilly underwear.
While fathers, husbands, boyfriends sheltered by the door
Guarding their wallets against the storm.

*Eileen Michalik, Abergavenny, Wales*

## MY LOVE

If I could conquer time,
I'd turn the hands back
To when I first met you,
But this time I'd know just
What to do.
I wouldn't let you walk away
Without a single word to say,
I'd shout for all the world to know,
I'd tell them that I loved you so
And then I'd take you for my wife,
To stay with me all your life,
To make you truly mine.
If I could conquer time.

*Eric Gilbert, Hengoed, Wales*

## TAPESTRY

This land of poetic history
Valleys steeped in song and rhyme,
Hold the secrets of our being,
Tenets of our age and time.
Centuries of industry and endeavour,
Carved deep into the face of our land
Has filled us with a sense of belonging
No stranger could understand.
Lives filled with wonderful sense
Of patriotism and faith,
Passed down through the ages
That no time can replace.
Father and son have fallen
But their lives were not in vain
Each adding strength to the tapestry
So our blood can rise again.

*Stephen Carlson, Cwmbran, Wales*

# WAR AND PIECES

He made no contribution to our talk last night,
His eyes were fixed in a plastic looking glaze
That made him seem five thousand miles away,
His arms too tired to lift to lips the beer going flat;
They told us he'd been caught up in a fight,
We wonder how he'll face another day.

He joined up as a soldier and his family was proud
They showed around the photos to their friends
The smile, the firm lip, the shoulders back.
He'd been to Ireland, now it's easier there,
To Cyprus too, he really got around,
And then the call for service in Iraq.

It's over now, his contribution's done:
He is alive, but not his mates who died,
And shock and sickness and a nightmare sleep
Wrap round him closer than plate armour ever did.
Count back the wars through history, one by one;
And here's another. It must make God weep.

*Bernard Johns, Chepstow, Wales*

## THE BLESSING AND THE GIFT FROM THE LORD

I received a special blessing from the lord here today
It was a very special blessing in a very special way
There was gift soon to follow in the way that I write
It was a very special gift it's the poetry that I write
The lord wanted me to tell you about the things that I have
said
About the blessing that he gave me as I laid so ill in bed
But when I did recover my poetry I did discover
I thank the lord for my blessing and the gift that he gave
That memory will be with me forever
That memory I will save
I will write it in a poem I will reveal it here today
It was a very special blessing in a very special way

*Pamela Williams, Merthyr Tydfil, Wales*

## THE CHILD ETERNAL

To survive the greatest loss of all
To keep intact your life and walk tall.
While all around you weep and mourn
And from your heart, a piece is torn.
To stand beside an open grave,
To bury there the life you gave.
To turn your back and walk away.
And wake and face another day.
To carry on with life's brisk pace,
To hide inside the tears that race,
To never show how much you care.
And others seem so unaware.
They think the pain has gone away,
And still it hurts, everyday.
To halt the grief and carry on.
The precious child, forever gone.

*Anne Jones, Mold, Wales*

# WOMAN THE ROSE

Mass of profound beauty
Surrounded by a hath of thorns,
For one to expect its beauty
First must overcome the thorns,

Velvet to the touch
Although painful to some,
Crimson red is the colour
But for what am I describing?

Mystify, arouse, bewilder,
Are few of her many traits
She'll allure persuade and beckon you
Into her frightful lair

Often dark and unsightly are her leaves,
But unravel these, to reveal the beauty that is she,
For she is a masterpiece, you won't ever be deceived
Because one there can only ever be,
Woman the rose.

*Maggie Williams, Caerphilly, Wales*

## SOUL MATE

I wasn't looking for you although I
knew we'd meet,
You walked across the room to me as
I sat in my seat.
You smiled your smile, held out your
hand and I put mine in yours,
That minute when our eyes met, it
seemed to last for hours.
I knew right then that this was fate
and we were meant to be,
because you took my heart and soul
and you gave yours to me.

*Pauline Perry, Neath, Wales*

## SUNSHINE AFTER THE RAIN

As raindrops patter against the damp window pane
I look outside noting the abundance of droplets gathering
However, soon the storm will be over
And sunshine again will show its face in the form of a
rainbow

Today optimism is in the guise of the sun
Overtaking what could have been a dismal day
Signifying better times and a beautiful future

Raindrops are God's way of saying teardrops are sometimes
inevitable
But there will always be cause for some happiness
So every time a droplet of rain appears on the window pane
It will be a reminder that they will soon disappear to be
replaced by a world of sunshine

*Marjory Price, Abergavenny, Wales*

## SHE WAS THE GIRL

She was the girl that nobody liked,
A loser, a loner, a freak,
A friendless frump, a stick in the mud,
A friend was all she would seek.
She was the girl, bullied and torn,
Thrown away and disregarded.
But where is she now, not bullied oh no,
For she is dearly departed.
She was the girl that took her own life,
Too broken and jaded to care.
Her want for a friend caused her sad life to end.
They miss her now she's not there.

*Natalie Boscott, Brecon, Wales*

## IN A WELSH VALLEY

In a welsh valley I was born
In the early hours before the dawn,
When thunder and lightening ruled the skies
As I opened my sparkling green eyes,
Upon a place novel to me
So rich in colour and bright things to see,
All the hustle and bustle that filled my sights
The shapes and sounds, the shadows and the lights.

I came forth into a world I didn't know
Unaware that in life I had to grow,
I was a product of love tiny and unique,
But not yet able to communicate and speak,
And today I still live in the same valley where I was born
Though much older now since I greeted that first dawn,
And it's where I shall exit in a state of repose
When the lord of the sky deems my eyes should close.

*Philip James, Merthyr Tydfil, Wales*

SEASONS

Still cold, but some warmth the sun doth bring.
Raising shoots from the ground, for now it is spring.

The hot summer sun brings vibrant colours galore.
From the flowers, the trees that grow more and more.

The leaves are now changing from orange to brown.
As the autumn breeze blows them gently down.

Winter brings rain, the wind and the cold.
It's the last season now left to unfold.

These months of the year, seasons we call.
You'll notice they don't really change at all.

Winter, spring, summer and autumn fall.
Winter, spring, summer and autumn an all.

*Kaye King, Bridgend, Wales*

*Dedicated to my parents Shiela and Len. Like the seasons I can always depend on them, whatever the weather.*

ART?

Shines like a crazy star
Emitting doubtful light from
One self-deluded as to a blazing talent,
This generated mainly by the driving force,
The overwhelming power of self-acclaim,
Nurtured by sycophant cries of: "Oh yes" -
Self-interest surely begets their critique?
Hopefully though, her lucrative offerings
To the world of art are tongue-in-cheek.

*Patricia Knowles, Conwy, Wales*

HOME

Dog with fire eyes
reflecting
fireflies
scars on his nose
from thorns
of a rose
barking at
every other dog
lost in the fog
of life
found a harbour
now
a home
with bones
on the floor
and by the door
a silver bowl
of water

*Ursula Bayer, Knighton, Wales*

## CHAIROPLANES

Breathless I swing
O'er the rim of the world,
Fingertips clinging,
My banners unfurled;
Wild exhilaration,
With uttermost dread,
Fear and elation,
Adrenalin fed;
Released inhibitions
All flung to the wind,
Far into the galaxy
Reckless I spin;
Past, present, and future,
All merge into one,
A final ascent to
The stars has begun;
Kaleidoscope colours
Where living has been,
Flash by in an instant,
The slate is wiped clean.

*Dorothy Neil, Cardiff, Wales*

MEMORY DRAWER

I'm sorting through my memory drawer
I try to keep it neat
It's a chore I don't mind at all
In fact it is a treat.
I read through our love letters written long ago
You always wrote such lovely words
Which said I love you so
Cushioned in a velvet box two curly locks of hair
Tiny little baby shoes
All wrapped with loving care.
The memories of our family growing through the years
Special little keep-sakes I see through happy tears.
Yes I'm sorting through my memory drawer
But I do it at my leisure
This drawer holds stories of my life
Each memory a treasure.
Photographs of times gone by
Each precious smiling face
It's all here in my memory drawer
These times you can't replace.

*Trish Elliott, Deeside, Wales*

HOPE

In death there's life
In life there's hope
In hope there's faith
In faith there's peace
In peace there's forgiveness
In forgiveness there's healing
In healing there's freedom
In freedom there is joy
And joy rests in eternity

*Amanda Hale, Pontnewynydd, Wales*

ONE MOMENT OF SHAME

Oh Lord I pray with you today all things are made anew.
The past is gone that lingers on inside my mind, for you
Have healed the hurt and pain that threatens loudly once
again.

'Tis I who brings back memories of sadness, tears and grief
And wallows in self pity showing utter disbelief
In who you are and where you are and what you did for me
When you sacrificed your only son and hung him on a tree.

He knew that he was helpless in the hands of evil men;
But in his eyes were hope and faith his spirit would
transcend
The shame of that one moment that time cannot erase
But proved his trust in God and turned it into endless
praise.
So may I take this moment when all seems dark and bare
To look into my saviour's eyes and see the answer there.

*Roberta Loveday, Cardiff, Wales*

# THE GRANDMOTHER CLOCK

When summer warmth chills out to cooler,
coloured days that speak of autumn, Our house
no longer opens her windows like arms to embrace
the freshly laundered sunny hours.
Instead her curtains like closing eyelids shut out the
wispy threats of winds and chilling icy blasts.
Then the warmth of hearth and candlelight,
of pot roasts, soups and toasted teacakes
pervades the now enclosed ambience
of each and every firelit room.

Throughout it all, the changes of seasons,
the children's departure into adulthood.
Behind the laughs, the sighs, the tears,
the memories, you hear one consistent,
comforting sound. The mellow ticking,
the heartbeat of the home; The stately
Grandmother clock. Quietly, serenely,
symbolising every second, every minute,
of each hour that contains the essence
of our home, our lives, our lifetime.

*Mary Howcroft, Swansea, Wales*

# THE LAST GREAT ADVENTURE

The last great adventure,
Ends when it begins.
No merriment or laughter,
No paying for your sins.
No meeting with the devil,
Nor angels stretching wings.
No speaking with St Peter,
Begging to come in.

No issuing of tuneful harp
Whilst at the pearly gate,
No worrying, with hand on heart
To learn about your fate.
No checking in the registry
To see how you've behaved.
No sending off to purgatory,
No waiting to be saved.

No hot reception down below
If you have failed the test;
Just darkness everafter
When you are laid to rest.

*Michael Marshall, Pontypool, Wales*

MEAN WHAT YOU SAY

Say what you mean,
Mean what you say.
You can talk to me
In any old way.

Doesn't matter to me
Whatever you say
Say what you mean
Mean what you say.

*Marvin Hughes, Cardigan, Wales*

DEMOCRACY, THE TRUE DEFINITION

Innocent, angelic, all the desirable qualities
Until they have power under their hands,
Then the guise is ripped back and hidden agendas
revealed.
Then corruption falls on the land.
Vampire like fangs protrude over smirking lips
As the power gushes straight to their head.
Little do their adoring public know
The old definition of democracy is dead.

All stands to be today
Is a right to wash your public in blood,
To grasp your supporters in your barbaric hands
And throw them in caverns dug in the mud,
To diminish your voters to prove a point:
They shouldn't be so naive in the first place,
To take a country under your rule
Then leave the world without its trace.

*Keighley Perkins, Cardiff, Wales*

## GRANNY'S SONG

My granny's favourite song, a maudlin air no doubt,
Made a major point, a crucial one, of what this life's about.
If I can help somebody, she'd sing then yet again
Incant the loving words, my life will not be in vain.

Oh granny dear, your time is gone, and many a tear's been
shed,
Not just for you but also for your ideals which are also
dead.
Because looking now it's hard to see the folk whom you
admired,
The kind who helped, gave all they had, to others who were
tired.

They're gone and been replaced by those whose only word
is me,
Whose lives are dedicated to themselves and only feel truly
free
When surrounded by belongings which define their selfish
lives,
Surveying from their vantage points my granny's ideals'
grave.

*Torquil Cowan, Holywell, Wales*

BLEAKLOW HEAD

It is spring,
but snow still lies
between the thighs of cloughs
whose fingers run along the spine
of the Pennines
until the high peaks are reached.

*Ivan Johnston, Welshpool, Wales*

AGGRESSIVE

Fingers raking,
Tongues slashing,
Bending in, space invaded,
Distorted face,
Missing teeth,
Constant, no rhetoric,
Doors bang, sealing key,
Safe secure, panic button.

The voices begin
You long for the conversation
That is not yours,
The missing people that say what
They should,
Pictures blend with surrounding darkness
Curtains twitching, eyes itching.

The things you cannot do.

*John Bennett, Cardiff, Wales*

## THE RAINBOW

Across the clouds in the mixture of day and dark,
Where there is haze in the sky and the boundary isn't
sharp,
Where above there is sun on one hand,
And on the other, there is dark and cloudy land.

Yet even in the city do I see,
The most admirable thing that could be,
Yet amidst the day and dark and unlike its nature,
Does it stand very bold, sharp and clear in its stature.

There it stands, the mighty seven bows,
Whose streams of colours across the visual world flows,
Yet as I towards it move in the train,
The further it shifts in sunshine and rain.

I try to approach it with speed,
But away it moves with the same lead,
It stays far from all.
Yet beautiful, fair and still it stands untouched and tall.

Can such beauty remain far from all?

*Shalin Parekh, Haverfordwest, Wales*

BABYSITTER

Dark, lonely mindless mum,
Thick clouds burst and pour.
Her fake appearance, her decrepit hand.
Reaching down, depths where she shouldn't go
Into unfamiliar land.
My mother's pride.

*Kim Johnson, Connah's Quay, Wales*

THE POWER HOUSE AND THE PANDY RIOTS

So long ago, nineteen hundred and ten,
Hard times for striking miners then
Seven thousand stormed this citadel
Men and their wives, their children as well.

Police, mounted, on foot, with truncheons attacked.
"Send troops," they demanded, "we need to be backed."
Provoking the looting of sixty four shops.
Far famed Pandy riots, response to those cops.

The strike dragged on for a full, hard year.
Its cost to our people starvation or near.
Strikers forced back without gaining one jot.
Waste and great sacrifice, like it or not.

My father worked later in that power house where,
High on its switch board with its spiralling stair,
His flick of a switch stopped any machine.
Once the sole goal of such violent scenes.

*Owen Vernon Jones, Tonypandy, Wales*

NEVER SMILED

I never liked Jack Walts
Never smiled, always wore black,
Black bower, black riding boots.
Grey flannel shirt buttoned to the neck, he never smiled.

Rode a small black pony,
He tall thin, long legs almost
That dragged the floor as he rode.
Two black crossbred sheep dogs
Trotted behind as if tied, No he never smiled.

Lived alone, solitary, run down cottage.
Looking through the window once;
Flagstone floor, large tables few chairs,
Long knife sticking from a loaf on the table.
Scraps on a plate, a mug lay on its side
Tealeaves still within No wonder he never smiled.

When he died, he died alone
Solitary as was his life.
His funeral few came, few knew he had died
Poor sod, those who saw off didn't smile,
No nobody smiled.

*Derek J Morgan, Aberdare, Wales*

EVENING PRAYER

The bleak river, large and melancholy
Affronts the many water birds;
They shrink like small idolators
Before sad icons.
A rough wind stings the late air
With a sharp tang.

Fishermen rub shoulders
With the inclement weather, pursue
Their solitary trade in a wilderness world,
Standing like monks bereft of prayer.

Time stands still.

I probe the edgy shallows of memory
Tokens of recall and loss,
Sifting faded pages yellowed
And blemished with blurred images.

I wait for answered prayer
But western clouds shut out
The phantom signs, darkness
Blanks the press of dreams.

*John Christopher Evans, Swansea, Wales*

# TEARS

Through all the traumas
That come my way
In the shelter of God's arms
I will safely stay

I will stay strong
For God will be near
Through all life's hurts
He will wipe away my tears

I will not fear
What will happen through the years
For God will protect me
And wipe away my tears

And when I grow old
And death draws near
He will hold me close
And wipe away my tears

I will no longer hurt
I will know no more fear
For the warmth of God's love
Will have dried all my tears

*Moyna Lydon, Llangammarch Wells, Wales*

# ODE TO DANIELLE

Your father called you sparrow
A scrawny little thing
With bright brown eyes a-sparkling
Like a bird who'd lost a wing

Your hair was short and tufted
Your body thin and long
You weighed four pounds ten ounces
Not really very strong

Your heart was small but perfect
And your determination true
And you were a little fighter
I just knew you would pull through

For nineteen years I've watched you
Your bright eyes big and brown
Your hair now past your shoulder
It's amazing how you've grown

I gave you lots of love, dane
And still will as time goes by
No longer are you a sparrow
But my beautiful butterfly

*Rosemarie Parry, Newport, Wales*

PAINTING BY WORDS

An artist has canvas and oils
Capturing sights and views with skilled eye
While over blank paper with pen
Empty mind staring hopefully at the sky

Will words flow like colours off the palette
A keyword a phrase something to start
Jigsaws of letters consonants and vowels
Express feelings from deep in the heart

A ditty about our feathered friends
A gull on a wing, lark soaring
Verses of jungles and ventures
Somewhere in the distance a lion roaring

Pick out a theme a story
Somehow the words tumble and fall
Onto paper once empty, blank
A verse of duty honour answering the call

Too many words now
Clear the clutter over elaboration
End up with poetry precise
A story of heart and soul collaboration

*Anthony Hillier, Port Talbot, Wales*

# THE DARK SIDE

Nobody knows exactly when
the seed was planted in her brain.
It grew from day to day and then
drove her mad, nearly insane.

The vicious monster gathered strength,
the nagging doubts, the bitterness.
She started building a great wall
to hide her torment and distress.

Drowning her sorrows did not work
because they are good swimmers.
They resurface with a vengeance,
in this game there are no winners.

All words and deeds are questioned,
those closest suffer most.
More bricks are laid, the wall gets bigger,
alone she fights an eerie ghost

And when the last brick was put in place,
dark, nothing, she might as well be dead.
No bridge, no lifeline to escape
and then she drowned inside her head.

*Marliese Porter, Monmouth, Wales*

# MURDER MOST FOUL

She was an awful nag, my wife, I'd had it up to here,
I was going to get rid of her, slit throat from ear to ear.
Then I thought about the mess, the bloodstains on the floor
And knew it must be different, 'cause mess I do deplore.

I thought and thought day and night, but still no answer
came,
The real reason of course, I didn't want the blame.
I'd have to leave a puzzle for the local CID,
A puzzle that led everywhere except of course, to me.

And then at last the answer came, just how to kill my wife,
I'd poison her, the nagging bitch, I'd do it with a knife,
A good sharp knife was what I had, all I'd ever need,
To poison her once and for all, that's how I'd do the deed.

The police, of course, knew it was me, however much I'd
lie,
But couldn't it work out at all just what had made her die.
Poisoned with a knife? It didn't just make sense,
So I told them how I did it, how could they be so dense.

I waited 'til she'd had a shower, her rear was taut and bare,
I knew just what I had to do, the answer was right there,
I took the knife from off the shelf, and with a graceful flick,
I stuck it where it had to go, gave her arsenic.

*George Kaine Baker, Swansea, Wales*

64

LINDISFARNE

A mystical, majestic skyline,
Appears through the dawn mist.
Forget-me-not blue hues of summer,
Wash over land and sea.
One salt encrusted causeway,
Laid bear by the retreating waves.
A visitor's passageway, to the Holy Isle.

An eerie silence prevails, broken only by the
Distant cries of scavenging gulls.
Cuddy's fortress erupts from its rocky base.
Across the briny wasteland the pilgrims walk.
A gradual pace unfolds, allowing contemplation
And prayer.

Overawed by its historic past.
Overshadowed by its presence. Each wanderer
Slowly climbs the serpentine passage,
To enter the inner peace.
The presence of those passed,
Envelopes your whole essence. A spiritual
Dawning begins, allowing belief and hope to reign.

*Annie Morrisey, Betley, Cheshire*

*Dedicated to my husband Chris, the eternal optimist who makes
my world a better place.*

**Annie Morrisey** said: "I have been writing since I was a teenag-
er and have had various works published. I draw influence
from my work as a make-up artist and through my travels with
my husband Chris. I also draw creative inspiration from artists
and sculptors, especially David Hockney and Tony Cragg. One
of my ambitions is to have a book of my poetry or monologues
published. I have compiled several collections of poems, influenced by my work and travels. My literary heroes are Jane
Austen and Alan Bennett. Poetry allows you to express yourself
in a way you may not be able to verbally."

## PIP

Pip pip pip pip pip
Was that a pip?
Pip pip pip pip pip
Who was that who pipped?
Pip pip pip pip pip
Oh, here comes Lisa Jayne
Pip pip pip pip pip
Now we know who's pipped

*David Jacks, Warrington, Cheshire*

## A SIGN OF THE TIMES

They planted trees, put benches too
Come to the park, take in the view
Monuments built as a lasting treasure
For generations to come there'd be hours of pleasure
That's what they said it's meant for all
Walk the dog or bring a ball
They didn't reckon with bikes speeding over the grass
Or the fires that blaze, or the broken glass
The gangs that gather to bully and drink
Who don't care what's around them and don't stop to think
That they are the future whose children will grow
In a place that they ruined and will have nowhere to go
Live and let live and have some fun
But leave something for others when your day is done.

*Dawn Hough, Northwich, Cheshire*

*Dedicated to my family and friends who share my life, the ups and downs but especially the laughter. I thank you.*

MUSING

Now I'm awake I must say
Welcome to a brand new day
The oncoming winter fast approaches
We must hold no reproaches
Birds and flowers, new mown grass
In your senses evermore last
Trees and bushes dancing with ease
Shedding their leaves in the autumn breeze
This beauty which is soon to fade
To bring the snows and rainy days
Later to march onwards to fresh spring parades

*Celia Cholmondeley, Warrington, Cheshire*

WINTER CANVAS

A bleak winter morning a sky of grey
A lone bird hovers like a bird of prey
Hovers - and - glides - in the currents of air
A glider pilot on wing without prayer

There's a rustle of wind the last leaves fall
Some glide like the birds then on letting crawl
Some - like winter butterflies - flutter in air
As wind shakes the trees which now are quite bare

Winter storm comes along painting the trees
There's beauty in starkness snow starts to freeze
The moon lights the landscape sparkles the snow
Illumines a canvas no artist could show

*Liz Standish, Warrington, Cheshire*

ECLIPSE OF THE MOON

You may have been eclipsed, but not in grace,
the sun which eased the shadow of our earth
across your beautiful insouciant face
blocked out by this old world that gave us birth,
cannot be gazed upon with naked eyes
in spite of his importance and his heat,
and lovers do not seek him with their sighs,
although the source of light, he is not neat.

But you dear moon in newness clear and bright,
hang like an epsilon of purest gold,
or in your fullness cast a modest light,
although men's feet on you have set their hold.

And now in rare eclipse the shadow shows
a faint blood gold that like an ember glows.

*M Munro Gibson, Winsford, Cheshire*

**M Munro Gibson** said: "Poetry is my main interest. I have
to share my work with other people and to read their
poems. My subjects are usually nature, people, faith and
astronomy. I have been published in many magazines and
anthologies over the past 40 years. my most recent collec-
tion is *Flowers on My Doorstep*. This 120 page book may be
obtained from me. Price £5, but there is a concession for
senior citizens who need pay only £4 towards costs (both
prices include postage). Please order from M Munro Gibson,
Thornley Villa, 213 Crook Lane, Winsford, Cheshire, CW7
3EG."

## ONLY FOR BARBARA

I love you
I love you
It's a promissory note
All a pulse
Like a beacon
In a follicle of light
Burning stillness
Blazing white
Waters reach in ardent flight
Still the beating of my heart
Touching
Waiting
Watching
Wanting
Only you

*Philip John Savage, Macclesfield, Cheshire*

*Dedicated to my wonderful wife Barbara, mother of Alistair and Antony.*

JUST A THOUGHT

The sky is dark
The lights are shining bright
The wind is blowing
Now it's snowing
I am on my way
Cold and hungry
Lost in thought of things
I could not buy
Like diamonds, pearls
A dress that swirls
Just a thought, just a thought
To go to Spain would be nice
Just a thought of the past gone times
When times were good and
Thoughts were real
There was laughter and cheer
All through the year
In the past gone times.

*Edna Fallowfield Jones, Chester, Cheshire*

OUR CHILD'S BORN YET GONE

Our child's born yet gone.
Hospital windows
Are cold Asphyxiation.
Am I always tiptoed here?
Longings chill choke hold
Leaves me dangling, arms loose over
This snow field sunset.

*Damian Mitchell, Crewe, Cheshire*


FOR OUR VAL

The time was 3.15pm
The afternoon was done
The evening crept in quietly
Today has been no fun
Everyone was pleasant
So kind and so sincere
The church had been quite busy
At this beautiful time of year
We do not know or understand
Why she left this life
Her time with us has been cut short
Severed with a knife
This person we all love and miss
Did not know the impact that her
Death would kiss
Her existence was not valued
By all who knew
We need you by our side today
And from the day you flew

*Kathryn Butler, Warrington, Cheshire*

## WARKLEIGH CHURCH

Latch click. A meditative space,
Indulgent light, compliant air.
The words begin to interlace
But will a poem replace a prayer?

The southern aisle is brightly lit
By jewelled lights within the cames
(So states the visitors booklet)
Of Messrs Heaton, Butler, Bayne's.

The ends of medieval benches
Create a screen beneath the tower,
Medallions, milords and wenches
Are carved within a leafy bower.

The grace and regularity
Of gothic vaults above the nave
Impose a metric clarity
Upon the words within the stave.

*John Evans, Altrincham, Cheshire*

PLASTIC BAGS

True. Those who hang up plastic bags to dry
on the washing line are mental, half there ...
In the sickening hour of night, without sky
or hope, fearful of touching the smooth skin

of ... a plastic bag. There's nothing in the game
you should know (try baseball or basketball
or simply play with a skull) and there isn't a name
in the pursuit ... half there, mental.

But searching ... searching, that is the main thing
and not finding. Nearly dead with hate-smoke
you would commit treason to know how to sing
or live again provided you could dissemble.

But Mr Hadzihasanovic stuffed
his newborn baby into a plastic bag
then wept at the graves of his ancestors ...
He played the game but he never ruffed.

*John Crotty, Warrington, Cheshire*

# I HEAR THE SOUND OF THE POURING RAIN

I hear the sound of the pouring rain,
Nothing's ever going to feel the same,
Without you here by my side,
You've left me with nowhere to hide,
I hear the sound of the pouring rain,
Give me something to control the pain,
The pain I've felt for losing you,
You're supposed to be here, I need to talk to you,
I stand by your grave feeling mild and bleak,
And a pearl tear falls down my cheek,
They start falling like the pouring rain,
Are things ever going to feel the same?
Then all the tears they wash away,
I realise you're here every day,
You're still there in the back of my head,
Your body's gone but your spirit's not dead,
You're still there telling me what to do,
You're making sure I don't feel blue,
The sun has come out again,
Everything suddenly feels the same ...

*Nicole Broad, Plumley, Cheshire*

I'M SORRY

I'm sorry I couldn't be,
What you wanted me to be.
I'm sorry my mind was somewhere else,
In a world of my own, I hid,
From your demands, your questions and your lies.

I'm sorry I couldn't do,
What you asked me to do,
A question so deceitful and untrue.
I'm sorry that it seemed like I didn't care,
I'm apologising for the neglect you said I put you through.

I'm sorry that the scars cut deep inside my heart,
And that life seemed so much easier,
When we were apart.

I'm sorry that you hurt me,
I'm sorry you weren't true,
I'm sorry it had to end like this,
I'm sorry ... aren't you?

*Gemma Connell, Wilmslow, Cheshire*

## LAST SHIRT

Forlorn in wicker linen bin
That final shirt carelessly thrown,
So prematurely leaving me
Despairing, desolate, alone.

Buried my face within its folds,
Faint waft of tangy aftershave
Reviving memories bittersweet
Long months since you went to your grave.

*Jenni J Moores, Northwich, Cheshire*

## RAIN, SWEET RAIN

The happiness of waking up each morn,
Opening the window to a brand new dawn,
Who cares if it's raining and the skies are grey,
It adds to the beauty of another new day,
I just love the smell of earth after rain,
Like it's making everywhere fresh again.
I lift my face to catch the raindrops
Whilst on my way, to visit the shops,
There's pleasure in the summer showers,
As they fall to freshen trees and flowers,
Or a thunder storm with the rain bouncing down,
And the lightning flashing all around.
To see rain hitting the window pane,
When you're sat in the warmth,
As it comes down again.
Though sometimes we're gloomy -
There's always tomorrow
Because after the rain, surely sunshine will follow.

*Barbara Ellison, Warrington, Cheshire*

## ARMISTICE AT ASDA

Suddenly aware
of clamour in the air,
babies complaining,
older people feigning indifference
as wristwatch fingers creep nearer
to the promise we must keep.
Market pronouncements,
intercom announcements
and then - the clock.
Eleventh hour is sung
and mercifully peace is rung.
Still, still,
silent now as death incessant
we stare at shelves,
thinking how to dignify ourselves
and then, as seconds slip away,
we cannot help but think
about the day, the dead
who now can only sleep
and then, in Asda,
all recall and weep.

*Gill Pomfret, Moore, Cheshire*

## TO MY CHILDREN

An inheritance so precious, the embodiment of joy,
Two pretty little daughters, and the cutest little boy.

The years have passed so swiftly, it took me by surprise,
It seems like only yesterday I heard your newborn cries.

I remember every milestone, they are safely set apart,
Forever etched indelibly, in the diary of my heart.

From tiny tots to adults, the time has quickly gone,
First sweet smiles, first tiny tooth, the memories linger on.

That special scent of baby, your skin so soft and new,
My love is all encompassing, my children, just for you.

Evoking deep emotions, from happiness to pain,
But oh to turn the clock back and do it all again.

I would never say "I'm busy, just run along and play,"
But patiently and gently make the most of every day.

More time to sit and listen, fulfil each childish need,
Make the priceless gift of children, an inheritance indeed.

*Diana Burrows, Weaverham, Cheshire*

*Dedicated to my children, with all my love, Joanne the feminine one, Julie the tomboy and David, uniquely himself.*

A SECRET PLACE

Deep inside my mind I go to find a secret place.
No one knows what goes on there by looking at my face.

One day I could be sailing away across the sea.
Another time, I'm with the Queen; she's pouring out my tea

When feeling low, I brighten up as soon as I remember
The night I danced the hours away, one wonderful
September.

Then, soaring through the sky I go. I feel so light and free,
While gliding slowly down to earth. It's great, just being me

My secret place gives me the peace and quiet to succeed
In shutting out the restless world, when space is what I
need.

I can be anything I wish, or go off anywhere.
Make up stories, re-live times I wouldn't want to share.

So, while the heaving masses push and struggle with life's
pace,
I simply smile and spend some time within my secret place.

*Eve Armstrong, Warrington, Cheshire*

# DEPRESSION

Do you walk in shadows
Where others walk in light?
And do you lie there sleepless
In the middle of the night?

Is the cup half empty
No matter what they say?
For all their reasoned view-points
It will always be that way.

Do your dreams just crumble
Like paper in the rain?
And people talk above you
And never see your pain.

Do you always stand alone
In the middle of the crowd?
'cause no-one tries to reach you
Or talk to you out loud?

You can climb the mountain
From valley to the peak.
Then take a look around you,
You are the one you seek.

*Jane Parker, Churton, Cheshire*

STANDING AT THE WATER'S EDGE

Standing at the water's edge, reflections dancing far and
wide.
Reflecting on a memory, remembering how things used to
be.
She can feel the sun on her skin.
Feel the heat it emits,
as it glows like a fireball,
burning a hole in a sky that expands ...
Further than you or I could ever imagine
More than you or I could ever begin to understand.

Water is lapping at her feet, forcing its way over the glisten-
ing sand.
An intrusion into her confusion.
An unwelcome host,
A ghost of her past.

Standing at the water's edge, it's time to turn around.
The reflections vanish as the sun disappears.
The memory is pushed aside.
She can feel a tear as she walks away
She lets it fall and she doesn't look back
there is no turning around ...
And she says goodbye to the ghost of her past.

*Diane Stanley, Northwich, Cheshire*

SEASONAL GREETINGS

May this day be filled with surprise
Especially when you open up your eyes
Remembering you during this special time
Roasting the turkey and looking ever so fine
You're the one who makes at all fun
Celebrating the birth of God's gracious son
Holly wreaths and warm mulled wine
Radiate festive feelings, throughout our time
It's a time for peace and goodwill for you
Sending seasonal wishes, hoping they come true
Thanks for everything, you have done this year
May your days be bright and filled with cheer
After all you really are the best person I know
So for you Santa says, Ho, Ho, Ho.

*Annette Smith, Chester, Cheshire*

CHRISTMAS CAROL

Fair number, fair number of showers around.
Some falling, some falling as snow on the ground
It's Christmas it's Christmas as every one knows,
Choirs singing, bells ringing nativity shows

The children, the children are smiling with joy
With presents held tightly they sing to the boy
The infant eyes laughing smiles back in delight
Angels in heaven cheer this wonderful sight.

His mission, his mission to save one and all,
Let's listen, let's listen and answer his call
Our saviour our saviour is with us today,
Let's all bow before him on this Christmas day.

*Brian Perry, Hyde, Cheshire*

I THINK ALOUD

I work, I play
I talk, I say
I walk away
Yet another day

I play with fire
With skips for hire
My friends I admire
I buy a spare tyre

I mumble things
I ring those rings
A choir boy sings
A microwave tings

I think aloud
A lion is proud
I scratch aloud
I have once frowned

I itch my hip
I lick my lip
My tea I sip
My pants I rip, I am a freak.

*Anthony Clements, Wallasey, Cheshire*

A FRIEND CALLED SANDRA

When someone asks me "who is kind?"
Your name always comes to mind
When trouble and despair abound.
You're the one who comes around
to hold me up in case I fall.
When no one else will care at all
So when they ask me; what is true,
I say, the love of a friend like you.

*Sylvia Quayle, Maryport, Cumbria*

Born in Brampton **Sylvia Quayle** has interests including knitting, poetry, crosswords, bingo and computers. "I started writing poetry when I worked in Preston. A friend encouraged me," she pointed out. Aged 58, Sylvia works as a carer. She is married to David and they have two sons, one daughter, three granddaughters and a grandson. "My biggest fantasy is to win so much money that my husband doesn't have to work any more," Sylvia added.

DOES PARADISE EXIST?

The wind is talking, the sun is burning
The birds are laughing, the tide is turning
The swan is posing illuminous white
Even visible in the dark of night
A tuneful song is the only thing heard
Uttered perfectly by a beautiful bird
The ducks they waddle along the waterside
Before setting sail on the gentle tide
The dark comes and brings with it the night
I say goodbye to this perfect sight
As I leave I hear a whisper say
Paradise exists and I saw it today

*Laura Boustead, Kirkby Stephen, Cumbria*

A LETTER, ASTRAY

He took another laboured-breath and then,
Heavy-handed, lifted pen to page,
He'd started once then started once again.
Dreaming your reaction, and trying to gauge your rage.

The letter sat six months upon his sideboard, next to gas
bills, library books and junk.
From time to time he'd think about its contents, move it to
the breakfast bar and then,
Forget it in a fog of work and money, as deadlines came
and went and passed him by.

It wasn't till the autumn that he took the time,
To open once-again his fortnight's work.
And reading it one cold October's dawn,
Then burning it that same October's eve.
He dreamt of all the good he could have done,
And all the smiling eyes he'd never see.

*Christopher Hall, Carlisle, Cumbria*

# THE AIR IS STILL AS THE NIGHT

The air is still as the night, I hear your echoing peace,
The star which twinkles, in the sky, like a candle at the
feast.
How can we speak of love, for what to quantify?
It's shielded by the image of what? That we have to sneak
about and lie?

To live we all have to question, from a boy to a man,
How we answer, is that destiny? If so is there a plan?
For the moment we are born, is it right to assume,
That the gift which was granted, we have the right then to
consume?

The child in the arms of its mother, doesn't ask to be loved,
it's its right,
For the man of whom I am speaking, doesn't give up with-
out a fight.
And of all mans failings, there is one which we all seek,
And that is to live together with love, or is that being weak?

*Dawn Graham, Barrow-in-Furness, Cumbria*

# THERE SHOULD BE PEACE

Christmas is coming once again
Yet still those bullets fall like rain.
For food and shelter there's still a need
So many wars fuelled by greed.

There is little we can do or say
We turn our backs and walk away.
We walk away from the beggar in the street
And return to our homes warm and neat.

Will we see the nativity play
And follow Christ for just one day
Will we eat our turkey and enjoy
The birthday of that baby boy.

He tried to show us how to live.
How to others we should give
Throw out the bad and leave the good
But we are humans and only wish we could.

*Angela Robinson, Carlisle, Cumbria*

## SILENT NIGHT

That Christmas-time, I held your hand,
We sang a carol of a silent night when all was calm and all
was bright
Then off I went to fight a war that no-one wanted.
Nights of lonely fear stormed by as
I guarded palls of darkness and could not stop my fears
From dancing round my head, nor the trembling of my
finger on the trigger.
No-one heard the unseen noises in my mind until the night
that all my mates were torn apart.
A silent night, all was calm until the terrorist gave his life
to send all us to hell.
I alone came home outside a wooden box,
No fanfare for me
No flag, no Union Jack;
A funeral for them
Yes for those who could not speak.
With politicians, top brass and drums, of course
But all I saw was you.
And as you drove my tears away
We held on to that silent night and all came calm and all
was bright

*Brian D Lancaster, Cockermouth, Cumbria*

## MOSH

Mosh - it is a modern word
I found it quite by chance,
It is not one that I had heard -
Its meaning is to dance.
Not dancing in the ways of old
But violently colliding,
Jumping up and down (I'm told)
Deliberately misguiding.
Rock music is the catalyst
For this very strange behaviour,
Although the young they do insist
It's cool to be a raver.

*Julia Dent, Kirkby Stephen, Cumbria*

## AN ACROSTIC

How shall I tell thee of my greatest love,
Unspoken until now to all but she?
Since first we met whilst wand'ring o'er the lea
Both know this comes with guidance from above.
At first mild interest, cooing as a dove;
Next passion builds, we scarce restrain our glee.
Down in the woods, we kiss beneath a tree
As close as fingers, nestling in a glove.
No passing fancy this, we are agreed -
Devotion cannot live a life of sin -
We choose to make our vows in front of all.
Inside a year our rings confirm the deed
For with one name the world knows we are kin.
Entwined for ever, true love does not pall.

*Richard Clark, Penrith, Cumbria*

CROSSWORDS

Crosswords. Without them where would we be?
From involved cryptic clues not easy to see
To the simpler crossword easier to sus;
Without exception they draw all of us.

I was first taught to decipher hard clues,
Get onto the wavelength of those who confuse
With their obscure clues which fox us somehow,
By a colleague who patiently showed me how.

It was a very important part of our day;
Even now I wouldn't have it any other way,
To study the Telegraph crossword clues;
I still do the crossword before I read the news.

Though I rarely manage to finish, I must tell,
As well as cryptic puzzles, I like equally well
General knowledge puzzles which test the brain;
There's usually one answer I cannot obtain.

We might see a paper someone's laid by
With an unfinished crossword, so we have to try
To complete it, determined it will not us bamboozle,
The elusive-clued, mind bending crossword puzzle.

*Marlene Allen, Penrith, Cumbria*

# A MATCH AFTER SCHOOL, NOVEMBER

Ruefully I watch the boys troop off their field,
clack and clash of bootstuds on an asphalt path;
communal sweat steaming from sodden shirts,
cheering team to team, formality before the bath.

That whiff of smoke which tints only an autumn dusk;
laughter of excited girls biding their time;
sky already shaded down to rose-flecked gold
behind tall filigrees of sycamore and lime.

Clear railway noises heard beyond the town,
a certain sign of frosty nights in store;
sharply poignant scents of trampled grass
as earth reverts to winter mud once more.

Nostalgia's song plays irresistibly,
word-perfect down the corridor of years;
sound and taste and smell combine to touch
a chord of young excitements, ageing fears.

My throat is almost hot again with laboured breath
for swift incisive breaks I almost made;
my blood is stirred by tries I almost scored
and memories of epic games I almost played.

*Brian Campbell, Wigton, Cumbria*

FULL BOWL

Just imagine peace and love and lots of mega fun
Is it really hard to think that heaven's in the sun
Through the fields of space you'll get there when you die
Or if you got life wrong you're born again to cry

Zion is the way, we'll all get there in the end
You've got to know the key, it's no good to pretend
Faith in God and religion lends a hand
The centre of a star, this is the promised land

Moons and planets first, you'll see how they all formed
Allah's magic works from the time the first man yawned
A most merciful creation, life and death to all
See we're all equal playing with the very same ball

The power of the lord touches all the same
Hostile minds burn out for they play a very sad game
The universe is vast, but small to divine power
Everlasting bliss bringing light to the darkest hour

Open your heart your mind, body and soul
God will take care of you, he will fill up your bowl

*Ben Almond, Burnley, Lancashire*

**Ben Almond** said: "I was a patient on ward 18 on section 3
when I wrote this poem. I think it's positive and very spiritual. I'm versatile with poetry and my next book contains
approximately 100 poems with different topics. The more I
write the better my poems become. I've noticed this over
the last six months. Some of my work is targeted at young
people to hopefully deter them from drugs and crime. My
other poems include politics, psychiatric illness, fantasy
and many more. I hope *Full Bowl* will entertain you."

NUMBER ONE

He was always number one, a title owned by few
He ran a full sized narrow boat, often he ran two
He was the owner, steerer and engineer
And cleaner and agent too

His pair would take coal on the "Jam Ole Run"
Two narrow boats full that's seventy ton
Atherstone down to Southall wharf
Boiler coal for Kearley and Tongue

He unloaded manually, no conveyor belt or crane
Load up with baltic timber, swedish ore or grain
Back to keep the Midlands working
Then start from Atherstone again

Number ones have left the scene, working pairs have gone
But boats still move around the cut, trade still carries on
Bagged coal for boats and houses
Sold by a number one

*Brian Capps, Clitheroe, Lancashire*

## NIMROD'S BEER GLASS

Over there in corner dark
There is Flo and Fred, a lark
By the bar stands Phil in thought
His girl a new frock she has bought

By the door slinks fiery Jim
Punched poor Eric on the chin
At the table sits uncle Joe
Stumbles home he's lost a toe

Standing close is Nancy Sike
She goes cycling on her bike
By the toilets stands Lucky Jim
He has a funny way with him

Leaning up against the wall
Flipping heck he's 8ft tall
Little lady like a pin
Every Friday has a gin

Mighty Hunter why do you sigh?
In your beer glass you do cry
They know quite well we had a row
Will Sheila forgive me anyhow?

*William Smyth, Lytham-St-Annes, Lancashire*

**William Smyth** said: "I was born in Pisces in 1940. I am a retired aircraft engineer who writes short stories and verse as an additional hobby to gardening. I am described as a literary eccentric. I am married with two sons and two grandchildren, Sophie and Joshua. I can be found at william@defor.demon.co.uk. My most notorious book is unpublished, *Florence Swiftly.*"

WHITE WORLD

White world, glowing bright and clean
Crisp and even, nothing mars the scene
Orange berries, dark green glossy leaves
So still, it seems that nature barely breathes

A flash of red as robin comes to feed
While a shy doe looks for fallen seeds
The fox lies close upon the ground
His breath rising like a steamy cloud

The stream trickles beneath an icy coat
Ducks now slide where in summer they did float
No dragonfly will settle upon the frosty reed
Or children with their jam jars catch tiddlers - later freed

Yet the joy of winter is here for all to share
The purity of colour, visible everywhere
Take a walk and see the wonder of this land
Your world changed by natures invisible hand

*Patricia Spear, Burnley, Lancashire*

ROOTS

This isn't real
You know it isn't, brother
How could it be?
Mountains, we're inside you
We play our instruments to nature
We'll improvise if we can't find the notes
We've woken up the trees, mother
What else can we do
But continue?

*Jenny Lomax, Chorley, Lancashire*

SEPTEMBER SONNET

A young mother
Who doesn't bother;
A child in a pram;
Each has the other;
Neither will or can
Remember
It's already September.
They laugh and chatter;
What does it matter
That leaves start to fall,
And some already lie dead?
Days start to pall;
Glory days are ahead;
Nothing matters at all.

*Geoffrey W Lever, Preston, Lancashire*

PICTURE FRAME

There you sit upon the shelf
A memory behind glass
Always there
To bring a smile
To the saddest soul
A memory always there
To be seen
By all who dare glance your way
They'll see the smiles of bygone days
The laughter clear, but silent
A moment of reflection
A smile
As times frozen is lived again
You'll always hold a memory
For all to see

*Oliver Waterer, Fleetwood, Lancashire*

**Olive Waterer** said: "I have been writing poetry for about ten years and I also write short stories which are in the horror genre. I have had a couple of my short stories published. My first short story was published in a works' newsletter for a hotel where I once worked. Since then I have pursued my writing and I have now just self-published my first novel with Pen Press which is titled *Triplets* and will be available soon from all good bookshops."

ONE LOVE

I do not need a card dear
Nor do I need a rose
For the love we have between us
Gets deeper as it grows

Two hearts were joined together
And one golden one was made
Which is mine and yours together
With a beat that will not fade

I see you every morning
And I see you every night
You give a kiss so gentle
With pleasure and delight

After nineteen years of marriage
Your always in my mind
So my dear and loving husband
You're my only Valentine

*Susan Middlehurst, Darwen, Lancashire*

MOMENTS TO REMEMBER

There are moments in one's life to remember
To hold your sweetheart's hand and give it a gentle squeeze
To watch a smile spread across her face because of your
deed
Her pearly white teeth give you a message of love
Then she gives a little wiggle, followed by a giggle, oh what
bliss
And all of this followed by a lingering kiss

*James Barnes, Haslingden, Lancashire*

LEAVING

What web is fate about to weave?
For me when this my home I leave
I've tried my best to live with thoughts
That being in this house has brought
Although some happy times I've known
This now can never be called home
The garden with the trees and flowers
Glistening midst the April showers
Now lonely days - and lonely nights
When mortals - now beyond our sight
Like holy ministers of light
Ghostly shadows - oh so dear
Are around me - always near
I'll say a prayer before I leave
And ask for a blessing to always believe
I'll turn a page down memory lane
And try to learn to live again

*Marion Kaye, Poulton-le-Fylde, Lancashire*

## ENGRAVED LINE

All thoughts and wishes have gone
Just your love in my heart
Like a line engraved in stone

When darkness spreads at night
The candles of my hopes can
Be seen more clear and bright

If I were the dear of my beloved
I would live in her heart
Not merely near of my beloved

The stem of my body's weak and lean
But loves seeds in the field
Of my heart is ever green

This kind of perfume is rare
When air touches your hair
Then fragrance spreads everywhere

*Mumtaz Ali, Burnley, Lancashire*

# THE MORNING

Misty valleys swamped below
A concoction of hazy hills.
Trees looming out of the landscape
Leaning like drunken scarecrows.
Fields full of ominous pools of water
Reflecting the watery sky,
So beautiful, so menacing

*Maureen Williams, Gisburn, Lancashire*

# THE FAIR SEX

Why are we here?
Why were we born?
So men could scorn
And ridicule the female sex.
Do they really think we are feeble and complex?
Only fit to grow seeds in our comely womb
From girl to old woman in her tomb.

No the years have changed
Our ideas and way of life.
No more work, drudgery and strife.
We are a person to be heard
Not close your mouth, don't say a word.
We have brains as well as love
The time is right to remove
Doubts, and show we are an important
Part of this world
It could not survive without us.

*Iris Tennent, Barnoldswick, Lancashire*

## LIFE CAN BE A BITCH

I want to throw this week away
Last week I felt that I could cope
But now it's got beyond a joke
I've had as much as I can take
Who says life is just a piece of cake

Let it all out, just have a rave
I am positively through with being brave
Give me the high life I simply crave
I will no longer be your slave

I am going to burn all of my bills
And take off up into the hills
No one will ever find me there
The rain will wash away my cares

I will be surrounded by nature's beauty
So softly contained
throughout the country
One day I will grow wings and fly
Feeling the freedom of a clear blue sky

*Christine Dickinson, Preston, Lancashire*

THE BARGAIN

"I will lend you this glorious earth" said the Lord
"You must willingly care and lovingly share in its beauty
and riches to reap your reward"

But if hatred and greed should ever prevail
Pollution should spread and harvests should fail
Then again from the garden
Which grew for your birth
Mankind shall be swept from my long-suffering earth
And while she recovers in heavenly care
You will learn, in remorse
How to love and to share

*J E Offord, Southport, Lancashire*

POTENTIAL

There's a boy from the ghetto
That no one cares to get to know
With a dirty face and ragged clothes
People just walk by looking down their nose

But what they don't see is the boy inside
The one that is being forced to hide
Due to the fear and hate surrounding him
And the firing guns dumb-founding him

He's a flower lost amid a wilderness of weeds
And the chance for freedom is all he truly needs
For he's a rough diamond that has not been found
He is a king that is yet to be crowned

*Natalie Rowlands, Skelmersdale, Lancashire*

# FRIENDS

Sunset boulevard sat in my backyard
Summer's here it's time to cheer
But no one's around and not a sound
How can this be, it's time to be free
So I pick up the phone and call up Jerome
But he must be out 'cos nobody's home
So I call Tony, Vicky and Gemma too
But no-one's in so what do I do
See how Nic's doing, he's usually in
But he says that he's busy doing something
Whooh, the summer meant to be the thing
But somehow I just don't fit in
What's happening, what's this, am I missing something
And with that the phone starts to ring
It's Kyle, and you can't help but smile
An invitation to a club with plenty of style
And when you get there everyone's there
All your mates dancing with dates
The summer's here everyone cheer
And everyone does 'cos they're all glad your here

*Anthony C Griffiths, Rawtenstall, Lancashire*

THE JOY OF WORDS

Poetic words of meaning have that certain ring
It strikes a beating heart with the wish to sing
A haunting melody that encloses the soul with peace
A fine wine slowly sipped in a small taverna in Greece
Time ferry-hopping to beautiful islands leave a deep sigh
The sweet memories of a holiday romance in days gone by
The wonderful new sight of a heavenly landscapes view
Visions of first spring flowers peeping from soft fresh dew
In natures own blessings bestowed so visible in all things
The exquisitely sheer beauty of fragile butterflies wings
What could be more perfectly poetic on the sensitive ear
A moment of joy shared with the shed of a happiness tear

*Dawn Prestwich, Lytham-St-Annes, Lancashire*

POETRY IN MOTION

I sit with pen in hand
Putting into gear my mind
Hoping the right words to find
Pen flowing on the paper they land

Will it be fantasy or fact?
Whichever, it must make an impact
Capture your attention from the start
Maybe pull a string in your heart

We all have a story to tell
And we hope we tell it well
We want it to be a success
To become famous we confess

*Elsie Ryan, Skelmersdale, Lancashire*

DAYBREAK

Let there be light and there was light
And the light sent the darkness away
And the light was called day

Slowly the light brightened the sky
It covered the earth and washed the night away
Lighter still yet lighter, daybreak had begun
In eerie silence and in misty grey

The fading stars they seem to lose their glimmer
Receding in the dawning of the day
Moving into far celestial reaches
Gently paling in the abyss on their way

The daylight lights up every corner
Opening up a brand new day
Soon the skies will change its colour
Changing to blue from a misty grey

Soon the sun will start to rise
And everything will awake
How good it is for me to see
The dawning of day break

*Edith Smith, Haslingden, Lancashire*

THE SAUSAGE TREE

I really wish that I could see
A wonderful, beautiful sausage tree
A sausage tree swaying in the breeze
That blows around my knobbly knees
With sausages growing in all different flavours
Hanging on branches for me to savour
It really would be a wonderful sight
Seeing sausages growing at such a great height
Then falling down with a very loud bang
To land by the edge of the cola pond
Near to the bushes where the french-fries grow
So I really wish that I could see
A wonderful, beautiful sausage tree

*Colin Foe, Blackpool, Lancashire*

IF

If I could be a guardian
to each and every child
I'd stand like a pillar
for they would need no place to hide.

If I could be a light
I'd touch each tiny heart
I'd keep them far away from drugs
And the influence that harms.

If I could change the world
I'd sprinkle it with love
And nothing dark would ever
touch the people that I love.

*Angela Priest, Skelmersdale, Lancashire*

SECRET DEPTHS

Amongst fertile thriving hills
An unknown cavern hides
Concealed in the denseness
Suppressed in time

Embracing, the verdant hills encircle
Luxuriant in summer foliage
And as the deep gully deepens
Streams and trickles whisper
Secrets
of a time gone by

Hidden depths of darkness darkened
Down the black, not blackened pit
Grey whispers, golden flickers
Withered faces, chink, clink, amass, accrue
Accretion for the depraved insatiability

Within this melancholic, leafy dell
Now resplendent in sunlit shadows
The secret waterfall whispers yet
Of loss and greed undisclosed
Of an underground concealed
Veiled by the rolling hills of time

*Gillian Hesketh, Little Thornton, Lancashire*

LOVE WHICH NEVER FADES

No longer there but still I talk
And feel she always listens
As rain pours down on trees all bare
Their winter branches glisten

No longer there to touch or speak
Her words, her voice I hear
Wise and strong they never fail
I stop and feel her near

All through the good times and the bad
Our sharing was unique
And still we bond together
Such love we have no need to seek

Her face I often see, but
How I long for her to speak
And love so strong it never dies
Rendering me humble and meek

A song only she loved, I weep
Her sayings I convey to others
And she'd say many times before she went away
"We always miss our mothers"

*Clifford Chambers, Blackpool, Lancashire*

GREAT GRANDMA

A little lady sitting there,
Her back is straight against the chair,
Her hands are thin like porcelain,
A fleeting look of high disdain.
In a punt on the river Thames was she,
At Queen Victoria's Jubilee.

Her feet down leafy lanes have trod,
She's close to me and close to God,
She conveys thoughts with just a smile,
She likes to nod a quiet while.
In a punt on the river Thames was she,
At Queen Victoria's Jubilee.

*Eric Dodgson, Lancaster, Lancashire*

STREET LIT JOURNEY

The lights of a town glitter greater than stars
And the headlamps ahead glow as fire on Mars
Signs illuminated a clear, crisp white
Cats' eyes watch like owls, giving little light
A milestone marks an all new town
And in the night all roofs look brown
Stars upon garden trees shining
Bright with Christmas cheer
Car reverses, shudders to halt
The destination near
On their return the car will get
Back on track
"Greenacres leading to Acremount" the letters stare bold
and black.

*Sophie Wenborn, Clitheroe, Lancashire*

# WHY DID THE SUN GO DOWN ON US?

Where has the sun gone?
Has something gone wrong?
Is it July or November?

Is it summer with autumn mixed in?
People wondered with a grin
Though we saw the sun in June
Is it simply out of tune?

The weather was cold, wet and windy
We could not go out in a dinghy
And people got in a shindy
For the sea seemed choppy

You would see it on TV
Of people being rescued
The weather girl nearly drowned
From the rough and choppy sea

The weather man did his best
To keep the Scarborough cricket test
From going under with the rest

Tomorrow could be a better day
We all head the weather man say
Sun is on the way

*Constance Price, Nelson, Lancashire*

# THE HARDEST PART

It's not the fact of dying
We come of age then leave, no denying
But with knowing you, I don't want to

You see it has taken most of my life
To know you, and make you my wife
Before I go, allow me to lament
I need to before I rest where I am sent

Sometimes it seems funny, like it will never end
Then from my bed I see my only friend
You have stood by me when I have been wrong
You still laugh when I sing a song

Days have passed, nights have slipped by
But our love for each other, no-one can deny
Do you know the hardest part
I want to leave you my heart

*Stuart Whitham, Blackpool, Lancashire*

PERFECT

Perfect in every way the chair in the hallway stands
cushioned with the kiss
Through the velvet cotton, the smell of the scent of love
The pattern silk shoreline like shimmering of bright light
meandering from heaven

Egypt of the Nile swarms the universe taking the world at
large sending love to every living soul
The day awakens where truth unfolds and the scent of love
still stands in the hallway, the pattern silk shoreline
shimmers through the crust cracks in the rock's outer
layer
Silk-dried the wood but the rotten creased velvet expands
into multitudes of bright beams of the sun's rays

The second jewel swarms the land giving the one with the
two hearts, of the beaten tracks
So hard to find swarms the seashore twilight hour, all in
one star. Many a moonlit star
Still stands in the hallway, the pattern, silk shoreline
shimmers through the crust cracks in the rock's outer
layer.
Silk-dried the wood but the rotten creased velvet expands
into multitudes of bright beams of the sun's rays, twilight,
she's the one with the letter perfect in her heart

*Janet Hosler, Prestwich, Greater Manchester*

Born in Bury **Janet Hosler** has interests including walking,
writing and art. "I started writing poetry five years ago and
my work is influenced by life. I would describe my style as
thought-provoking and I would like to be remembered for
my beautiful vision of the world today," she remarked. Aged
37, Janet has an ambition to be a full-time author. She has
two children and has written a children's book as well as
several poems, several of which have been published. "My
biggest fantasy is to live by the sea," Janet added.

WHERE ARE YOU MY LOVE?

Am struggling to find the pathway to reach you
I know you left the blushes of your cheeks in the rose-
bushes
Your smiles are dropped in the smiling snow-drops
You left your youth in the spring blossom
You threw the colours of your life to decorate the rainbow
Here, I am bending and bowing for you my love
Where are you my love?

*Anantha Rudravajhala, Middleton, Greater Manchester*

CONGESTION AHEAD

Crawling tentatively, heeding warning
Of heavy congestion, early one morning
The limousine, with windows tinted
Purred alongside, like a cat having sprinted
And caught his prey, and lay contented

The uniformed chauffeur, driving with care
Wearing dark glasses to protect from the glare
Grimaced and frowned as he stared downhill
At vehicles snaking almost to standstill
Their brake lights flickering a fiery quadrille

Concern for the passenger, travelling within
The luxurious interior, he stroked his chin
And glanced in the mirror, anxiety to save
Towards the celebrity, a smile he gave
She returned the smile, with a royal wave

*Kathleen Frances West, Bolton, Greater Manchester*

# WAITING

Waiting
Excited. Keeping looking at the clock

Soon I'll have my arms once again around my family
Keep looking at the clock

One more minute nearer, I'll kiss and hold them so tight
They are the one's who light up my soul each day and
night
Keep me together and give me a reason to live

Keep looking at the clock

Loving them more for each second that ticks
Waiting with my heart beating fast
Want to hold them forever this time, make it last

Keep looking at the clock

Soon I'll see their smiling faces and the love that glows
Surrounding their heavenly but earthly figures
Only to each other's eyes can this glow be seen
Because we are a family and know this love is real

Keep looking at the clock
Excited
Waiting

*Jo Rainford, Leigh, Greater Manchester*

## LINDOS

We have a picture from our holiday
on our bedroom wall.
It reminds us of those carefree days,
without worries or problems at all.

It's rained non-stop since we've been home,
I detest this autumn weather.
The picture makes me fret and moan,
let's emigrate together.

In our album I've stuck the snaps
along with each memento.
I look through the pages, but alas
I'm even more depressed, and say so.

What can we do to bring some cheer
the rain churns our lawn to gravy.
When a daughter phones, early next year
we're to have a brand new baby.

*Valerie Wyatt, Stockport, Greater Manchester*

Born in Brentford **Valerie Wyatt** has interests including spending time with her grandchildren, writing, knitting and designing. "I have been writing since childhood and my work is influenced by everyday things, usually ones which make me laugh," she pointed out. "I like to make people smile and my ambition is to have more of my work published." She is married to David and they have three sons. "I have written short stories, children's stories and hundreds of poems, some of which have been published," Valerie added.

LIVING IN FEAR

I walk down the street, it's dark and it's late
People stumbling drunk - oh what a state
Nervously I approach a gang of girls
Dressed up to the nines, high-heels and curls
Suddenly one of them shouts at me as I walk past
Surely if I ignore them the shouting won't last
But suddenly I feel an almighty pain
And I think to myself "these girls are insane"
Then slowly the darkness becomes so light
As I close my eyes so firm and so tight
My mind starts to wonder at what I might find
Maybe all this hurt is in my mind
Then I wake up to find I am in my bed
The pain I was going through was all in my head
And then I think one day this may come true
After all living in fear is what we do

*Kelly Morgan, Swinton, Greater Manchester*

MY DAD

I loved you dad
I know you knew
But you never said
You loved me too

I know you cared
But it's not the same
You never said it
No one's to blame

The years we lost
We never made right
Now you are gone
I am alone to fight

The tragedy that put a wall between us

*Marie Kay, Bolton, Greater Manchester*

*Dedicated to my friend Mervyn, in deep appreciation of his endless encouragement to keep going and rise above my tragedies.*

Born in Bolton **Marie Kay** began writing when she was nine. "I was feeling wretched because my mother and brother had died," she explained. "My work is influenced by life's experiences and I would describe my style as deep and varied. I would like to be remembered as someone who was kind and never lied or stole anything." Aged 60, Marie is a former radio operator with an ambition to prove that it isn't just famous people who get their writing published. She is a widow and has written two novels, a sitcom and a biography as well as many poems, several of which have been published.

DREAMING

Softly, stealthily and silent
Thoughts of you filter through
Until my being is suffused
With the sweetest memories of you

Like a child clings to a breast
Or a plant soaks in the rain
With hunger my body seeks for you
And the ache I feel again

So strong, yet breathtakingly gentle
My mind like a whisp of down
Falls in a moonlit pool
And allows itself to drown

*Alice Campbell, Harpurhey, Greater Manchester*

THE MAN IN THE WIND

He comes as if to devastate, rip up trees by the roots
She feels the pressure around and through her
Rest and not fight the weight of his ardour
Now he means business - this is serious
Full attention is given to the question in hand
Whether to blow over, around or through her
Or off on another venture

He comes in gusts, blows hot, blows cold
And as he blows she stands her ground
And as the arms of the woman enfold him
He is where he is meant to be
He can't give up - but no fight left
He succumbs
To tenderness

*Barbara Jardine, Oldham, Greater Manchester*

A LOVE POEM

Watching the moon
Laughing at its pale face hiding
Behind the smoky clouds
We held hands
In an unearthly radiance

Our first love scene
My fingers were electric on
Your cool skin

Tonight you will go home
Miserable to leave me
And I will sleep
Wrapped in the scent of you
The sound of you
Only a phone call away
Miles apart

*Eileen Hudson, Rochdale, Greater Manchester*

MY DREAM GARDEN

If I had one special dream
And my special dream came true
My dream would be about a garden
Designed for me and you

With grass as green as kittens eyes
And sky as blue as sea
This garden would be a wonderful place
For only you and me

The sun will shine so brightly
The pond will gleam all day
In our special garden
Where we can relax and play

The flowers swaying in the breeze
With colour everywhere
So if you see this special garden
You can't help but stop and stare

With trees as tall as towers
With birds as small as mice
This special garden for me and you
Would be like paradise

*Amy Hawkins, Leigh, Greater Manchester*

Born in Wigan **Amy Hawkins** has interests including writing poetry and drama. "I like to write poetry about animals and I would describe my style as coming from the heart," she pointed out. "I would like to be remembered as a happy person." Amy is a student with an ambition to be successful. "I have written stories and many poems, several of which have been published," she pointed out. "The people I would most like to meet are the authors Jacqueline Wilson and J K Rowling because they are such imaginative writers."

BEAUTIFUL LADY

Picture hanging in a frame
Beautiful lady, what is your name?
Lady from a time gone by
Into that time through this picture we pry
See the cut of her dress, her white silken shawl
As she gracefully smiles down from the wall
Dark silken hair
Skin so fair
Gracefully sitting
For the time so fitting
The artist into her life did breathe
And captured time he did weave
Each delicate brush stroke made life flow
Oh, beautiful lady, from long ago

*Sheila Baldwin, Wigan, Greater Manchester*

THIS IS WHAT I WANT FROM YOU

I want you to hold me as tight as you can

I want you to love me with no doubt in your mind

I want you to teach me everything you know
From the colour of the sun to the colour of the snow

I want you to show me love in the world
Show me the beauty of what we all hold
Peace and tranquillity in our hearts and our souls
Our minds empty of doubt and filled with love

I want you to love me with all of your heart
Be at my side and never part

*Greg Foley, Walden, Greater Manchester*

# THE KNIFE THROWER

I throw knives each night
At a woman who was once my wife
Years have passed since the divorce
Since then no intercourse
Of any kind especially words

She used to be a beauty in her day
But time has taken its toll along the way
Each night she stares eye to eye
As the knives go flying by
Towards her body

Her eyes are full of unshed tears
And I know in my heart
She fears
The one night when
The knife will miss

*Sheila Ellis, Prestwich, Greater Manchester*

UNTITLED

A cold hand reached out from the grave
And touched my face
It left a finger print of love upon my cheek
Though dead so many years
Her touch felt only a moment old
I thought I heard her voice calling out my name
Or maybe it was just a gentle breeze
Blowing memories through my mind
Because when I opened my eyes
I was standing alone in the rain
I walked home that night
I didn't want to listen to the taxi driver's happy chat
Or stare straight ahead in the English way
On a bus
I wandered down many vandal darkened streets that night
But if the truth be known
Any mugger would have met his doom that night
That night I felt her hand upon my face

*Peter Hewitt, Oldham, Greater Manchester*

BLINDING COLOURS

So blue was the sky
so green was the land
contrasting and
blinding my eye

Then it occurred
a little small bird
on wings unfurled
flew wafting a-tween
the blue and the green
and created: his world

*Tanya Sorell, Sale, Greater Manchester*

Born in Hamburg **Tanya Sorell** has interests including
reading and debating. "I started writing poetry as a teenag-
er to solve the problems of existence and my work is influenced by my aunt and grandfather," she pointed out. "My
work must always contain a thought and rhyme." Aged 84,
Tanya is a retired teacher with an ambition to help people
cope with their problems and give them a philosophy of life.
She is divorced with two children and the person she would
most like to meet is the writer Margaret Drabble to discuss
different trends in poetry.

TOMORROW'S PROMISES

The leaves are falling at the year's turning
And sound a plangent chord
Summer's lease is all but over
And winter whispers in the breeze
Through the still heart of the silence
The earth is held in suspense
And utters a plaintive breath
To quiet the souls of the animals
The past is in sepia tones like a photograph
To stir ineffable memories
And yesterday lapses into tomorrow
With promises of another year

*Peter Lang, Rusholme, Greater Manchester*

HIDDEN TRUTHS

Mirror, mirror
On the wall
Show me the truth
Display my all
Reveal my secrets
Portray my truths
Relate my lies
Be my proof
Unlock my inner sanctum
Discover hidden treasures
Shout out my loathing
Whisper my pleasures
Spill my contents
I've nothing to hide
Exploit my private thoughts
To you I confide

*Katherine Fish, Heywood, Greater Manchester*

LIBERATION DAY

We came to civilise them, not dictate
As newsreels invoked visceral images
Of past campaigns fought in cancerous climes,
We haven't learned a thing.

Oh that these eyes had not seen such slaughter
As we rampaged over ravaged landscapes
My honourable heart deceived me too,
Leaving them helpless and hopeless.

I still see my friends, of course,
In nightmares, consuming my waking hours,
Cursing and wailing like banshees
But who heeds their piercing cries?

My morphine mistress tends me now,
Her crisp white uniform bequeaths
An innocence long since lost
In this vicinity.

*Paul Burton, Stockport, Greater Manchester*

UNEMPLOYED

The drip, drip, drip of water from a leaking tap
Into a scum lined sink was barely heard
By the unshaven occupant of a discoloured armchair
Accessorised by visible springs.
Leaning forward slightly he strained to catch the voice
Of a thumb sized Tony Blair giving a speech
From inside a battered television set.

"That good-for-nothing twit.
I could do the job much better given the chance."

He voiced his opinion to an empty room.
Empty after all his friends and family had gone,
Gone and taken the chance
That everyone had been given.

He knocked a crushed beer can
Off an empty pizza box perched on the chair arm
And swore loudly as he finally realised
His mistake, he had been left behind.

He sighed and reached for the yellow pages
He really couldn't afford to fix his tap...

*Elizabeth Holt, Bolton, Greater Manchester*

ROCK STARS

Rock stars all a singing,
Some look like they're from Mars,
Just why do they do it
Some break their guitars.

Rock stars with torn jeans,
Tattoos, leather and lace,
With long hair a hanging
And paint on their face.

Singing the high notes
They struggle and sweat,
To reach number one,
And then jump on a jet.

Off to America, Germany, Japan,
Touring with roadies in a big van.
Tuners and amps, lighting and mikes,
Fans follow in leather gear on motorbikes.

But they all make great sounds,
And just where would we be,
Without these great rock stars
Who set us all free.

*Mavis Ann Abrahams, Wigan, Greater Manchester*

CLAUDIA

Little boys play outside
Little girls play inside
With dollies
Whilst their fathers' cigar smoke
Raises like ribbons
Into the innocent blue air

Toy trains and toy soldiers
Plates high up on mats
Hopes that growth from shoulder to shoulder
Will last, for eternity

*Briony O'Callaghan, Withington, Greater Manchester*

THE CRASH

He called the emergency services on his radio
Scratched the roof with his other hand
"Oh my God, Oh my God," he said
Over and over and over again
As if all his pain was compressed into those few words
I couldn't see his fare, her side
Pinned by the bus into a "V" against the barrier
It took forty five minutes to free her, she lived
Another twenty for him, he died
There was neither panic nor screaming
Just quiet acceptance, quiet desperation
Even surprise
The scratching ceased first, next his prayer
Then three more breaths
Each estranged from the last
Orphaned him

*Pamela Igoe Hall, Rochdale, Greater Manchester*

NOSTALGIA

Looking back remembering
Searching out the past
Events that took place long ago
In our hearts will always last
Reminiscence with an old friend
About the bygone days
An item took down from the shelf
Such warm and friendly ways
The lyrics of an old song
The title of a book
Mother's home made apple pie
Fashions outdated look
A ride upon a steam train
A journey on a tram
A cob of coal, an old tin bath
A meal of bread and jam
This old world it keeps on turning
And as we journey on
Nostalgia will hold a special place
When all these things are gone

*Ian Hogg, Heywood, Greater Manchester*

MY WISH

Each hour goes by, the days do to
Sometimes very slowly
Hours that once were filled with love
Are now so long and lonely

Looking back the years have flown
Yet it seems so long ago
And to live each day when on your own
They do still drag on so

How do you cope when left by yourself
After a loved one has died
You pretend you are alright to everyone else
While on your own, you know you've lied

You feel so lost when out in a crowd
The odd one out among your friends
They laugh and joke, you do too
But it's a farce, you only pretend

If you were given three wishes
It's not money or property you lack
Family and friends do help you
But it's the loving happy times you'd wish back

*Eileen Waldron, Leigh, Greater Manchester*

# HOW LONG IS A LIFETIME?

How long is a lifetime? No one can tell,
Which as you'll agree is perhaps just as well
No one knows what lies ahead
Or if we'll wake up when we go to bed

Don't let your problems spoil this life,
It is easy to give in to trouble and strife.
Don't be gloomy and sit around moping,
All over the world there are people coping
With war and hunger and many horrors,
Volcanoes and earthquakes causing such sorrows.

Appreciate your friends and every loved one.
Keep on smiling or else you'll have none.

Enjoy the myriads of beautiful flowers,
Blessed by the sun and watered by showers.
Listen to the singing bird in the sky,
There is so much beauty to feed the eye.

Greet each dawn with joy and pleasure,
Realise this day is another to treasure.

*Jean Wood, Sale, Greater Manchester*

## WHEN I WAS YOUNG

How sad it is to have lived so long
There's no one to remember
When I was young
Days that slipped by
Like leaves on a stream
Eased into a lifetime as I
Worked out my dream
The highs that we shared
Glow on through the years
The lows we despaired
Often drove me to tears
Yet were powerless to harm us
Because somebody cared

But memories fade
When you're all alone
Choices I made
Were not set in stone
Now I scarcely recall
How it all used to be
When we were still small
And you remembered me

*Josie Carter, Atherton, Greater Manchester*

CROCUS

We hadn't seen the sun for weeks
Each day was dark and dreary
The air was full of drips and leaks
Everything looked dead and weary

Then one morning, brightly beaming
Through the glass into the room
The sun's sharp rays, transforming, gleaming
Lighting up the winter gloom

I looked out into the garden
And there among the greenish grey
Of last year's shoots, beginning to harden
I saw a flash of orange gay

Was it a label, wet and windtorn?
But it looked too fresh and bright
Its vivid colour glowing warm
Glinting in the morning light

The first hint of spring - a crocus
One of nature's neon signs that say
"Winter's death is merely bogus
Rebirth is not so very far away"

*Marjorie Pinder, Bury, Greater Manchester*

KEEPING YOUNG AT HEART

I had a good childhood when I was a boy
Living with nature and used to enjoy
Watching the tadpoles who lived in a pond
Turning into frogs and go hopping along

I still like to see them like millions of others
In their own way they became my sisters and brothers
I still get delight at the nature around
And the antics of nature which I have found

Perhaps there is nature in heaven as well
Then I could watch God's spirits for a spell
In my imagination like tadpoles, they will be there
A big head and a flat tail moving everywhere

Perhaps I could be a spirit as well
Swimming and flying over hill and dell
And even write poems about heavenly bliss
Sealed if my wife came, with a heavenly kiss

Making life perfect for her and for me
Free at long last for all eternity

*Jim Haslam, Rochdale, Greater Manchester*

# I FOLLOWED HIM

Betrayal, ridiculed, beaten, denied
Robbed of his life by elders who lied
Copious amounts of striated pain
Awarded by men with nothing to gain
Whipped with sticks flesh left his back
Legs and arms pounded until they fell slack
Body all lacerated till it went frail
His blood and his flesh drip from the flail
Cast from the city by those who lie
The chant from the mob shout crucify
Carried his burden through narrow street
The blood ran freely poured over his feet
Upon head resides a vicious crown of thorn
Skin hangs from his wounds not an inch untorn
Nailed to the wood drenched in his blood
Exhibited above, cross plunges down thud
In agony he writhes fighting the fight
Until man is forgiven he suffers his plight
Accomplished he shouts, loud as he can
He suffered and pained for the sin of all man

*Andrew Hughes, Moston, Greater Manchester*

## THE CHURCH GATES

Now blue and as good as new
Fencing off our rhubarb patch
They were found lying in the grass
There at the back of the church, they did sit
The path was widened
They would no longer fit

What could they tell us and recall
The weddings and the funerals
In sunshine and in snowfall
The folks who trod the path
Wearing their best outfits
Or humble bonnet and shawl

A meeting place for neighbours
A treasured building once
But gone is its raison d'etre
No longer accepting its dogma
Folks keep their ethics still
And the church stands
Like a beacon on a hill

*Doris Thomson, Middleton, Greater Manchester*

TICK TOCK

My dad left me an old grandfather clock
It had a tick but not a tock
It never ever showed the right time
And at one o'clock it didn't chime
One day I stood it on mums old rug
I polished and oiled it and gave it a hug
Then I heard a tick and a tock and was amazed when it
chimed at one o'clock
I realised the clock had been sad
Of course it missed my mum and dad
So now every time I pass it
I stroke its mahogany case
Now it ticks and tocks and keeps good time
It chimes and has a happy old face

*Margaret Howarth, Tyldesley, Greater Manchester*

TOWNIE

Spray-mounted
And thumb-print
Embossed
Memory
Of the earthy
Taste of fire

And
Soul and
Love
And being

Blood-savoury
And
Devoured

*Paul Neads, Salford, Greater Manchester*

CHANNEL FOUR, SATURDAY, 1 AM

He sits, quietly contemplating
And waxing his own wordless image
With a veil of introspective
Art house excreta

Then it's all back to his, for some
Pretentious post match analysis
That no amount of well meant
Punditry or dumbing down
Is ever going to make a
Blinding bit of sense
To the bewildered
Prime-time loving
Insomniac

*Simon Bostock, Stockport, Greater Manchester*

CORNWALL

The rugged coast of Cornwall
The smugglers in their caves
That's what it was like in olden days
The fighting and the battles
The roaring of the sea
The pirates with their contraband
Are fascinating me
Jamaica inn folk gathered round
Drinking mulled wine
They could tell a tale or two
About this bygone time
It must be nice to recap
If only for a day
The magic memories of Cornwall
I think are here to stay

*Ann Noble, Stockport, Greater Manchester*

SHARED ADVENTURE

Steel blue sky, touching grey blue waters
Lapping against slate grey empty shore
The soft white surface of waves gently ebbing and flowing

Two young children making the most of their holiday
Laughing and shouting as feet splashed the icy cold
Neither would retreat an inch nor admit defeat by the
weather

Pink and white-stripped jumper, long hair caught and
tossed by the breeze
Blue top and shorts held up well above the knees
Faces grimacing and laughing two free spirits doing as they
pleased
Sailing a small boat and standing at the prow
Family heading out on the waves
Towards brooding dark clouds and distant hills edging the
sea

Parental awareness, allowing children to imagine and
dream
Capturing reaction on camera from the ships stern
A perfectly poetic moment in time this shared adventure
Learning to sail a boat

*Freda Grieve, Formby, Merseyside*

MUM AND DAD

I'm lying in my bed
Wide awake
Listening to the sound
That my parents make

Yells about my mum's new boyfriend
Fill my head
I'm sick of this argument
So I hide under the covers of my bed

They are still shouting at each other
Dad sounds furious
So I come up from the covers
Because I'm so curious

My mum hasn't seen me since that night
Her boyfriend was beat up by dad
He is going to court today
I've never seen him so mad

I've still not seen mum
I've only heard her over the phone
Now dad's been locked up
Never have I felt so alone

*Gemma Dutton, Rainhill, Merseyside*

# A MOTHER'S LOVE

There's nothing like that maternal feeling
It's a blessing in disguise
From the moment we hold them in our arms
And feel anguish from their cries
A gentle cradle to the child
The suckle of the breast
The warm feeling of comfort
From mother's heartbeat
As he snuggles into mothers' chest

"Now there baby, settle down
Mummy's here, no need to frown"
We walk the floor singing a gentle song
For we know he'll drift off
And it won't be long

He sleeps in his cradle
All cosy and snug
Content that he feels
His mother's love

*Amanda Johnson, Liverpool, Merseyside*

UNLOCKING OUR TRUE FEELINGS

Searching very deep inside
I walk through the wilderness of the mind
Cultivating those neglected seeds
Gathering the virtue, instead of over grown weeds
Our hearts they are gardens that are perfectly poetic
Analysing feeling, finding perfect meaning

*Tracy Costello, Liverpool, Merseyside*

HAPPINESS

Oh desperation, turn to dread
I cannot store it all in my head
Cloak me in a veneer so thin
Drawing every molecule through my skin

Coveting happiness so much
I try hard not to let it go
No weight, nothing to cling to
Oh, there is much, much more
My aim to guard that special store

If the weight becomes heavy
I do not care, too much happiness
Why do I have to take care?
Can it be weighed, is there
A balance due, too much for me
Too little for you

*Marj Kurthausen, Wirral, Merseyside*

MISCHIEF

Well, look at you, you little scamp
A doggy version of a tramp
Where did you get in such a mess?
I think I know, just let me guess,
Could it have been the field next door?
Just get those paws off my kitchen floor.
Well my lad it's a bath for you, before you come inside,
So no use hanging your head in shame
Or look for somewhere to hide,
Or look at me with soulful eyes and lick my outstretched
hand
And wag your stumpy little tail and hope I'll understand.
That little dogs just love to do, the things you've done today
It's part of being doggy, a part of "doggy" play,
Well I'll forgive you, just this once
But don't come close just yet
Not until you're clean and sweet
My mischievous playful pet.

*Martha Birch, Wirral, Merseyside*

REFLECTIONS, EARLY MORNING, CROSBY SHORE

Sea, sky fissured by first light
Dogs walking dog-walkers
Ships in far distance catch the light
Far beyond, Welsh mountains hover shimmering
And so much more is painted in my mind

*Penny Wilson, Liverpool, Merseyside*

WORSHIP

I have seen in some English towns
Seaside often, and swept by breezes
Churches standing solid and lovely
Stonework mellow and saturated with psalms
And carpets rolled high
And leaning against hallowed walls
Crude and colourful, and prices
Blazoned on card, thickly with felt tip
And I have wondered
If there could be a sense of God
In the touch of pale blue carpet
Or an urge to kneel down on the cloak of scarlet
Roughly unrolled down the aisle
And will the salesman perhaps
Surrounded by sacred spirits
Whisper some sort of prayer
As he closes the holy door on the stroke of five thirty

*Jean-Angela Smith, Liverpool, Merseyside*

# HATE MAKES THE WORLD GO ROUND

Hate makes the world go round
There's no more time for love
Focus has fallen upon disagreement
Who rules the heaven above?

Religion's caused a deadly divide
Throughout a dying world
No more time for fun and games
A gun for boys and girls

Mutilation, pain and death
Both in body and in mind
Is there hope for a hating world?
Is there hope for mankind?

Governments invest in nuclear arms
"Lets blast them until they're dead"
No more money for the NHS
Innocents die instead

"No more war" the protesters shout
But it falls upon deaf ears
The power that the government wants
Costs us all our tears

*Kim-Marie Fisher, Wirral, Merseyside*

FRATERNITY

If everyone was as kind as can be
The world would enjoy fraternity
Being kind is easy for a few
So why can't others be like this too?
People who are thoughtful will never be alone
Because they are too busy to sit and moan
To fraternise daily will make one whole
As this is uplifting for the soul
When fraternity is part of everyday life
It will eliminate sinful strife

*Thomas McCabe, Knowsley, Merseyside*

WHERE IS MY STAR?

Where is my star? I one time said
And gazed where uplifted night bled silver,
But there was not one for me
In that whole bejewelled company.

I wandered long through soul-set sands
Yet found no oasis in my tears,
But dunes of doubt and valleying fears,
The milling feet and toil-worn hands.

Yet borne upon unbridled winds,
Caught by the unceasing beat of seas
Comes yet the toiling sounds of bells
That beckon harmony and peace.

*Albert Pearson, St Helens, Merseyside*

# THE WIND

Underneath the burning sun
Or over the midnight sand
I can fly through seasons too
In every type of land
Sometimes I am whispering
Sometimes almost still
Sometimes with an angry force
Sometimes bound to shrill
I can only be one thing
Though varied is my name
And even though I fool myself
I always win the game
I cannot help this nature
But you will understand in time
Study me and catch me quick
Get to comprehend the sign
All that is, it's all out there
Wrapped around those pretty sighs
Would you be me, if you could dance
As well as I can, in the skies

*Christine Hale, Wallasey, Merseyside*

## THE SHARK

If you like bathing in the sea
Then you would do well to listen to me
The shark won't see a boy or a man
He'll just see a hamburger or a piece of ham
He won't need extra relish or extra sauce
Because he'll have your blood of course

First you'll be swimming, splashing about
And then his blue fin will start to stick out
He won't eat you whole but he'll chew you in chunks
And then with a burp he'll spit out your trunks

*Wendy Black, Liverpool, Merseyside*

## MY PERFECT PLACE

In time and space
In my mind behind my face
There is a place which is full of grace
With scenery so beautiful I could never erase
With sounds so harmonious they beat the perfect bass
The flowers and the trees have aromas to please
There's no way ever I could try to replace
I want to pick the flowers and bring them home to put in
my favourite vase
Here everything is pleasing and fine
I can walk life at my own pace
There's no need for me to run the rat race
She when life gets me down
I get up and pack my little case
And return to my perfect place

*Suzanne Strain, Litherland, Merseyside*

SPOOKED

'Twas a cold winter's day
In the churchyard dark and grey,
I saw a figure tall, dark and menacing
Wander amongst the gravestones, as the church bells ring.

And as I watch the mysterious form
I begin to feel so forlorn,
Which suddenly changes to spine chilling fear
As I see the figure in the churchyard disappear.

Frozen to the spot, I stand cold and alone
Not able to move and longing to be home,
What was it I saw that gave me a fright?
That can walk through stone and disappear out of sight.

Ghosts don't exist at least that's what I'm told
So what was it that left me so terribly cold?
Some might say that it's my mind playing tricks,
But why would I want to imagine men walking through
bricks?

*Lynn Kilpatrick, Liverpool, Merseyside*

# BEREAVEMENT

I was in a secure unit many years ago
I wanted a pet
The ward manager said "no"
In trouble and court, from Japan was bought a cyber pet
To be petted, and fed and cleaned
As I returned in the van, it seemed, shall I give it a name?
Things weren't the same
The sad news was broke, softly the nurse spoke
On a bifta I did toke
One of the staff tried not to laugh
"We've killed your Tamagotchi"

*Philip Johnson, Rainhill, Merseyside*

## ZANTONIA DYSTONIA

Rock roped and hook croaked the river rings of grinning
jinns
In swinging grins and swimming hymns of rustic trusts
and
Plastic husks where phantom fellows flout the gallows
against the straight
The shallow and the yellow of chasms raised against the
maze of rivetted maids and billeted nails were imminent
rails and minute snails shunter stops of stagnant mops in
pleasant shops and peasant hops where rich is mixed and
ditched
And stitched beyond the hitch of cleric clicks and relic
tricks of sunny suns and funny puns as harrowed flowers
ship the shade of narrow arrows and hour marrows to ease
the flame of metal showers and reptile flowers

*Meleeze Zenda, St Helens, Merseyside*

# A CHANGING SEASON

The season is changing
The trees are all bare
Gone are the flowers
To replenish next year
Some birds are all grouping
To fly far away
While the birds in the garden
Are all here to stay
The snow has arrived
Like a silver white shroud
Falling like feathers
From a grey heavy cloud
Sprinkling on branches
And blanketing the ground
Covering the hills
With not even a sound
We all know that this
Is not going to last
For the season will change
And dispel all its past

*Hilary McShane, Hoylake, Merseyside*

PHANTOM LOVER

I wait all day long for the darkness of the night
Because then you come to me and the world is bright
No one even suspects the love we both still share
A love that transcends all, so deeply do we care
We have pushed the boundaries to the limit
I think of you, only you every minute
The power of the mind is greater than we thought
Now we are rewarded with the knowledge we sort
I gave my soul so that you could stay in my heart
And now forever and ever we will not part
I conjure you to me and you always will hear
For us to both exist we have to be so near
I feel your gentle touch and it's heaven to me
My phantom, my lover who only I can see

*Ann Blair, Prenton, Merseyside*

ADIEU TO SUMMER

The wind has blown
The last of summer away
And already transparent wisps
Cling to the apple tree
Reluctant to release their hold
And disintegrate
Into a gossamer nothingness
Gently now the night unravels
Into dawn, the darkness shading
In the brittle starlight, fading
To a pink cheeked day
In the pale September light
My lover calls to me
Between the tangled branches
I can glimpse eternity

*Elizabeth Browne, Southport, Merseyside*

NIGHTLIFE

At night I escape to a different way
Of living to that which I live in the day,
It's a mad, mad world, full of confusion,
A mixture of horror, fun and illusion.
Adventures and mysteries, who knows what night brings,
I can fly through the air and all sorts of things.
Meetings with loved ones, gone long ago,
How they appear, I really don't know.
Sometimes I hear myself literally screaming,
Then I'm awake and I know I was dreaming.

*Janet Hagen, Killyleagh, Northern Ireland*

AN UNCHARTERED WORLD

In my ward of darkness, I often hear
The screams and moans, of my wounded comrades,
Yet despite it all, we still share a joke
And lose ourselves, in our nervous laughter.

In my locker, my shaving mirror waits
For a face I may never see again,
Not since that morning I stood in my trench
Looking at fear, in my weary red eyes.

The misty imprint of my left hand fades
On the window by my hospital bed,
The view is smeared, but soon it will be wiped
By the hand of an obdurate system.

*Paul Hutton, Coleraine, Northern Ireland*

## BOLD KENNEDY K McARTHER

When days grow cold and autumn gold steals over Derock's
Mountains,
The crops are in and round Drumfin, the stacks are bound
for winter.

Sometimes the talk round fireside turns to deeds of old and
further,
But none can can top that gallant one of Kennedy K
McArther.

The day was hot, the race was long, but nothing could
deter him for he pounded on, both brave and strong and he
left the field behind him
As he strode along he did belong to a breed that knows no
stopping.

First past the post he did coast,
Bold Derock's son has surely won
A place in sporting history,
Where only those who can oppose
And conquer all life's mystery.

So think about this gallant feat,
Hold high his name to further
That none compare with that debonair
Bold Kennedy K McArther.

*Samuel Coulter, Ballymena, Northern Ireland*

# OVERWHELMED

A romantic I may be,
But still even I am sceptical - this feeling can't last.
No one chance meeting could erase the past,
Stir notions of love in me again.
True faith.

Not I - queen of fanciful flings, inconstant things.
Too independent, too stuck in my ways, my lonely days.
Though seemingly determined in this lifelong quest -
To find the one who'll love me best.
Chance meeting or such celestine gift -
Have I glimpsed my destiny?

Still, all these constant thoughts considered, he remains
Invading my every day, locked deep into my brain.
Fortunate in my ailment, I quietly welcome it.
Overwhelmed - he loves me.

*Julieann Campbell, Derry, Northern Ireland*

## EMBRACING THE TEMPEST

In a frenzied lather of whiter than white foam
Remorseless waves make swiftly for the shore,
The puny sea defences are overwhelmed and powerless
As great cascades of water surge onwards and inland.
A small craft pitch poling in the tumultuous surf,
Tests the mariner's skillful navigation to the limit.
In the relative safety of a cliff top vantage point,
A watcher observes the froth and fury of the storm,
Her outstretched arms gladly embracing the tempest.

*Rose-Mary Gower, Treuddyn Mold, Wales*

## GREATEST FAN

Photograph clenched in your hand,
Gazed at it for hours,
Like a trophy it had pride of place in the room,
Taken everywhere you went,
A kick about in the park, it was there
Drink down the pub, as you got older, it was there
Since you were a boy you've been his greatest fan.

Wipe your face, holding your frail mother's hand,
You lifted the spade, dropped the earth
Threw down the bunch of roses, cried,
Gazed at the photo another few hours,
You were his greatest fan,
Just a memory, now he's gone.

*Kiera Patricia Byrne, Ballymena, Northern Ireland*

ALISON

So you thought you had seen
The last of me forever and ever,
And did you forget me?
As if that could be possible
And did it ever seem
While we spent all of our days together
We could have sat all night
To put the rest of the world behind us?

I want to break out of this spell
And get you out of my head
Once and for all,
You are driving me crazy,
Yet I am so content to feel this way.

Only time will tell
If I am going over or under,
So I might as well
Start putting all of the past behind me
Yet still I think to myself
Girl you always were really someone
But is this my foolish self,
That's making a big deal
Out of nothing?

*Derrick Alexander McBrier, Swansea, Wales*

## ONE FALSE STEP

I'm falling, falling, falling
Down into an abyss,
Surging down a fissure so deep
I never will be able to find my way out,
Am I sowing what I reaped?
This is punishment gone too far,
Far beyond one's mind,
What shall I do, who can help me
Or have I passed all cares afar?
Leave me to fall down, down, down
To my bottomless pit of pain,
Why help me, why care at all?
It's only reality I can't cope with.
Does reality only come in a dream?
I will not allow my falling
Come near you or your mental state,
It's mine to keep like a treasure
My abyss, my madness, my calling.

*Kathryn Evans, Llanelli, Wales*

# I BURIED A GOOD FRIEND TODAY

I buried a friend today, I had known her many years,
Always there when needed through good times and tears.
I knew her as a baby, watched her grow and bloom
So full of life and mischief, attentive eyes like moons.
Never cross or moody, full of love and cheer
Took life as it came, held no malice or fear.
As time went by the friendship grew.
Shared secrets just between us two.

Looking back those good years seem
Unreal, fragmented, like a distant dream.
Your sparkling eyes now dulled and waned
Sought help from me, but all in vain.
I gave you comfort, shared your pain;
It wasn't enough, death pulled in the rein.
My anguish remains but your spirit runs free.
Just a dog to some but a dear friend to me.

*John Dancey, Carmarthen, Wales*

HORSE

Are you aware as you lie,
Sunlight dappling the deep gold of your side,
In the lush green grass,
Are you aware as you flick at the fly with your velvet ear,
Rippling the sinews of
Your thick, warm neck,
Are you aware of your beauty?

A toss of the mane and proud women gasp with envy.
The arch of the neck spells nobility, no royalty could
match.
The drop of the head speaks of honour, not servility,
The sweeping plume of the musketeer.

You rise with muscle that would quell the brute,
Yet set in motion ballerina grace.
Rear and offer a salute to freedom
Causing the poet and the artist to despair.
Full gallop into symphony, the composer snaps his pen.
The philosopher weeps in the great depths of your eyes.

As you lean against the fence,
The light breeze lifting golden strands across your brow,
Are you aware of your perfection?

*Joan Conway, Holywell, Wales*

LAST ORDERS PLEASE

The flowers look so pretty
And the garden smells of rain,
The song thrush sings the sweetest songs
And can you hear the water as it gurgles in the drain

When your arms shall hold me,
I pray that you will see,
Not a flame that burns less bright
With the passing of another night,
Not despair and shame futility and pain,
But a light of joy knowing when that time has come,
You will the means employ.

The rain has come again,
The wind has wild ways and secret places,
How can you not love the rain.
There - the heron stands so still and stern,
His beady eye his lunch will earn,
Make another cup of tea,
The journey that I have to make
Is the only journey left for me.

*Doug Smith, Llandeilo, Wales*

PERFECTLY POETRY

Writing a poem is an art,
It's the way of expressing words from the heart.
The influences come from the topics that surrounded me,
That makes my feelings free.

When people read my poems,
The people make me smile.
A lot of thought goes into my work,
To wait for people's opinions, takes a while.

To make a poem rhyme,
Takes a lot of time.
Sometimes reading poems makes me laugh,
"I don't know why"
Other poems make me cry.

I enjoy writing poetry,
It's a hobby of mine.
Reading a poem is relaxing,
The aim of good poetry is making it poetic

*Leanne Victoria Evans, Port Talbot, Wales*

JANUARY PRIDE

January is a month of cold,
Nights dark, closed behind curtains -
Taking light from inside to make us bold.
Frost, stillness, sun melts the white away.
Shopping done, tired and freezing,
Coming home to warmth will make my day.
Birds need feeding, water for their beaks.
January doesn't think of them,
With snow upon mountain peaks.
A glimmer of spring, small shoots appear.
Giving hope of sun, warmth with every small spear.
Pushes its way through dark hardened earth,
To say God bless for all re-birth.

*Chrissie Taylor, Chester, Cheshire*


A VIEW FROM BRIGHTON STREET

What are they: light leaves in the sky
or simply feathered flyers?
They gather for the journey south
and land upon the wires.

I gaze at them a little while
against the greying sky,
and in the barber shop I turn,
idly wondering why:

the lilies of the field toil not,
the birds have free air rides,
and yet each month I must fork out
for a swift short back and side.

*Reginald Waywell, Warrington, Cheshire*

## MALCOLM

Malcolm is a taxi-driver.
Malcolm drives a cab.
He does the school run every day.
The traffic drives him mad.

He's cruising down along Hough Green
And everything is fine.
He grapples with a roundabout
and makes it just in time.

Negotiates the Grosvenor Bridge
And onward into town.
And then another roundabout
It's here he starts to frown.

The traffic's going everywhere.
There isn't any space.
He rants and raves and shouts a lot.
He thinks he's in a race.

And finally it's Sandy Lane
It's winter and it's dark.
He's stuck behind a minibus.
There's nowhere left to park.

*Ann Marie Whitehouse, Chester, Cheshire*

FLICKER OF SORROW

He says he feels fine.
He says he'll never die.
He still laughs and jokes and lumbers about.
And I'd laugh too,
If it weren't for that sorrow,
That flicker of sorrow in his eye.

*Megan Ingham, Sedbergh, Cumbria*

UNTITLED

You look at me
Hold my gaze
Blue eyes
Overwhelming
The light flickers.
I hold my breath.
You smile
And kiss me
Just a gentle touch
Soft and slow.
My heart races
Pounds and flutters.
Blue eyes
Light within
You feel it too.

*Jenna Fye, Whitehaven, Cumbria*

## MARKET VALUE

"Who'll start me at sixty? Sixty I have.
Eighty. One hundred. One twenty, forty, sixty.
Any more? All done? At one sixty?"
The calf looked up at the gavel's rap.
In another country he'd be looking for the matador.

"And the next one please. Lot forty two."
A photo-negative of the previous lot
Was dragged into the ring. Splay-legged,
Head hung, it didn't move.
"Start me then? Anybody?"

"Twenty to get it going? Let's not hang about.
Fifteen then? Ten to take it out?
Come on, I know Jack doesn't want to take it home.
It's got to be worth ..." "A fiver for it"
The farmers round the bidder laughed.

Jack, like the calf, had hung his head
Trying not to hear the jibes his neighbour said.
"So do I sell it?" asked the auctioneer.
A slow nod brought the gavel down.
Jack and the calf moved on.

*Geoff Hunter, Cockermouth, Cumbria*

IF LOVE WAS ...

If love was a smell, what would it be?
No doubt it would smell heavenly.
Maybe its scent would be sweet like a rose.
Just the right hint, which eternally flows.

If love was a vision, what would we see?
Something so beautiful like a crystal blue sea?
The colours would be vibrant, stick in your brain.
You would never witness anything the same.

If love was a touch, how would it feel?
As though an angel was hugging you, quite surreal
The touch would be warm, soft and tender.
You would melt, easily surrender.

If love was a taste, what would it be?
I think it would be something that would tantalise me.
Something as sweet as my favourite treat
It would, no doubt, make my heart skip a beat.

If I could have one wish, what do you think it would be?
I would wish for all this to be true for me.
However, there is one important thing missing from my list.
That is you. You're the one I wish to hold, love and kiss.

*Clare Bell, Maryport, Cumbria*

TIME GONE BY

Oh what a waste when we grow old
Remembering deeds in youth untold
In seasons green we laughed and played
No thought of time as youth decayed

All the hopes and dreams inspired
Now lay as dust, years expired
Turn back the clock, would that we could
To finish the tasks we left undone

Time laid weight on limbs each year
Only memory is crystal clear
Youth of today scoff at the old
What memories for them, as life unfolds?

*Chrys Valentine, Blackpool, Lancashire*

FIRE IN MY HEART

Put out this fire which is in my heart,
For I wish that I could be a part of you
In each and every way
For each and every day.

Being away from you sets me on fire.
All I keep doing is jumping like a live wire.
Our love is like a flame burning and hot;
Flickering when a gust of wind exposes itself
My love for you is like the walls of heaven;
Too good to imagine.

Our love will last forever,
In hope of our eternal flame
Always.

*Hannah Schofield, Blackpool, Lancashire*

ANIMALS ARE

The giraffe is kind
But the fly has a simple mind
The robin is dainty
The spider makes people fainty

Now the hyena is cheeky
And the tiger is sneaky
Flamingoes are beautiful
But the rat is very dull

Crocodiles are boring
While dogs keep on snoring

The cheetah spreads mayhem and disaster
But the lion is the jungles only master

The shark makes fishes demise
While the owl himself thinks that he's very wise

Rabbits like to live in the ground
But snow-leopards are never found

The elephants are nearly all the same
Whether Indian, African, wild or tame

You see animals are amazing

*Charlotte Bevis, Cleveleys, Lancashire*

## SCRUTINY

Heads so heavy
An unbearable strain
The pounding is numbing
How long will it stay?

The feeling reaching
Upward and upward
The taste, the memories
So slow in healing

To continue throughout
Insomniac nights
Insanity looming
Embracing fright

A task to conquer
Who has the strength
To be capable and able
The oblivious test

*Suzanne Jenkinson, Preston, Lancashire*

# INTOXICATION

They stand straight and proud
Adorned with golden curls

Grin like cheshire cats
Mouths open, baring orange sabre teeth

Clamour for attention
A feast for the eyes

Intoxicating fragrance exudes
Pervades the air, assaults the senses

A vision of Arabian nights
Sensuous silks, precious jewels
Oriental spices

The pure lily

Nothing in the world is arrayed
As fine as one of these

*Ann Sutcliffe, Burnley, Lancashire*

# ANNUNCIATION

Accepting as you were that day
Relying on God's mighty power
Pass down to us your steadfast trust
And guide us gently at this hour

Produce in us a hope that lasts
A quiet heart that's filled with love
The better to receive with joy
Whatever comes from God above

O Mary, you were greatly blessed
The chosen one of all our race
Not rich in wealth or worldly goods
But rich indeed in spotless grace

Please keep our names deep in your heart
Give consolation to us here
O lead us gently to your son
And pray for all to be sincere

We thank you for your word of "yes"
Though troubled you must at first have been
Protect us with a mother's love
And let us be like you - our queen

*Margaret O'Neil, Preston, Lancashire*

BANK HOLIDAY SUN?

The edges of the clouds are lit up by
The hiding bank holiday August sun

Way out in the east the grey clouds
Trimmed with this proof that the sun
still lives in the east

Now this sun rises above these dark
clouds and shines through the gaps in
the leaves of the giant silver birch tree

A magpie arrives on this scene looking
for some crumbs for breakfast

All these dark clouds are cleared from
the scene leaving it looking clean after
some overnight rain

The leaves of the giant silver birch tree blow
and a shower arrives again vertical gently
falling to the sodden earth, the light fades

The clouds gathering the sun goes in

*Margery Mahon, Preston, Lancashire*

IN AN EASTERN TEMPLE

White latticed walls reflect unclouded skies
Far distant mountains shimmer in the haze
And here one hundred thousand Buddha's gaze
In silence from the niche each occupies
Staring across the hills from painted eyes
While in the temple through the passing days
Saffron robed monks instruct in Buddha's ways
As in this place all doubt and discord dies

Tranquillity extends through every space
For here the fleeting hours seem motionless
And all earths troubles vanish in the mists
Unmoved, each enigmatic, sculptured face
Of the Lord Buddha stays expressionless
And only peace and harmony exists

*Mary J Baxter, Burnley, Lancashire*

## MY FRIEND

I have a friend to turn to
The best friend of them all
He helps me with my problems
And doesn't mind at all
I know he cares about me
For me he's always there
He helps me not to worry
My burden he will share
He puts my mind at ease
When I tell him my woes
For after I have spoken to him
All my worry goes
I could not live without him
It would never be the same
There are thousands just like me
Because God is His name

*Carmel Allison, Cleveleys, Lancashire*

SOUL MATE

The truest love is with you
When a thought just slips to mind
The truest love will warm you
When you see that face so kind
You feel its power embrace you, wraps round you like angel
wings
The truest love is in your heart and makes your spirit sing

The truest love will greet you
Two souls will lock and bind
The truest love will touch you
It's rare as rare to find
But when it's deep within you, much joy that it doth bring
It makes you feel as light as air, like two doves upon the
wing

The truest love won't leave you
It stays with you forever
The truest love won't part you
Your lives belong together
And when you find your soul mate, everything will be fine
And now that I have found you, perhaps you could be mine

*Andrea Davies, Atherton, Greater Manchester*

PICTURE DREAMING

I'm looking at a picture and it's where I want to be
I'm sitting on a terrace and am looking out to sea
I'm hoping for the dolphins as I'm by the pretty bay
Knowing that most evenings they usually come to play
I'm waiting for the sunset so I order some red wine
And as I watch the sun go down I'm feeling rather fine
I then request a menu and start to choose my meal
It all looks very tasty as Greek food has such appeal
I really am relaxing and I have a smile upon my face
I seem to have forgotten that I'm at home not in that place

*Jean Broadhurst, Stockport, Greater Manchester*

HOLIDAY OBSERVATIONS - PART 1

I arrived at the apartments and club house of Excelsia
One of many coach loads of sun seekers to accompany me
to my destination
It was late into the night and children lay sleeping
They wait for tomorrow to make themselves known
Overweight children rock back and to
On plastic sun beds
Tattooed parents watch
Unmoved by the repetitive noise of
Plastic against concrete
An 80s hits compilation plays sunshine and sandals
99 red balloons, eternal flame by the Bangles
Football
Big screen action
Just in case your chosen company
Loses their attraction
Older lesbians together apply sun cream attentively
Eastern men apply themselves needlessly
Western women judged, one to ten
By the bared chest that God put in front of them

*Stephen Mitton, Burnage, Greater Manchester*

LIFE

Life can be a drudge
Or life can be a stroll
The dice are thrown by the hand above
Who knows which way they'll roll
Take every day as it comes
And live it to the full
Be optimistic, smile, and life will never seem dull
Live life for yourself and help others if you can
Mould your own future, be the master of your own plan

*George Donnellan, Wallasey, Merseyside*

THE MENIN GATE

They roam the fields
Those ghosts of men
Who fought in that terrible war
They shake their heads and wonder
Why and what it was all for

Name after name on the enormous gate
Tells of the bodies they never found
While not far away in snow white graves
Their friends lie beneath the ground

I stood and watched by the Menin Gate
As the setting sun glowed red
Then the bugler came and shrilled his call
To bring the living to mourn the dead

*Elizabeth Porter, Eccles, Greater Manchester*

# WISDOM

Such a strange gift
That is given with age
It can't be given
Bought, traded or sold
You don't know when
Or how, it's going to come
But later on in life
When the lightning strikes
That bolt from the blue
This gift is given
And is special just for you
It's yours to pass on
But something you'll always keep
Treat it gently
And it will serve you well
To those you teach
In the following years
Through fun, laughter, grief and tears
Wisdom is the one thing
That holds no fears

*David Shepherd, Liverpool, Merseyside*

## HIGH HEELS

Her heels click a rhythm on the cobbles of street
She never fails to give a smile to anyone she'll meet
Her clothes are bright, her jewellery loud
She never is discreet
But what she sells, not gives away
Is wonderful and sweet
Her job's an old profession
Respected by no one
No certificates hang on her wall
No accolades are won
Yet she gives as much to commerce
As any banker you could meet
As her heels click a rhythm on the cobbles of the street

*Jacqui Dunne, Liverpool, Merseyside*